Published

He

ISBN N

1st

C000143354

Copies can be ordered from
www.henrypublishing.co.uk

or:

Henry Publishing,
23 Waulkmill Drive, Penicuik EH26 8LA
Midlothian, Scotland, UK.

Printed by  Tel: 0131 453 6643 Web: www.elevateyou.co.uk

Contents

Dedication

And the old man said:
"Our slavery was not life -
It was an unjust stain
that only equality will remove"

DEDICATION

The Enlightenment Abolished is dedicated to Reverend Robert Wedderburn. He was born into slavery in 1762 in Jamaica and died in England in 1835. He was the son of James Wedderburn of Inveresk, Scotland and Wedderburn's black slave, Rosanna. Robert Wedderburn was rejected by his father who turned him away from his house, Inveresk Lodge, which was bought with 27 years of slave-money acquired in Jamaica. Robert Wedderburn raged against the injustice and degradation of slavery. He was jailed in London for his anti-slavery protests. However, his father James Wedderburn lived out his post-slavery life, in great luxury in Inveresk.

James Wedderburn's house, Inveresk Lodge, now stands in Trust, in its whitewash splendour at the high end of a large tranquil garden, now open to all. Local historians speak graciously about James Wedderburn and his well-placed white descendants but, through either ignorance or omission, no mention is made of his 27 years as a rapacious slave-owner in Jamaica. James Wedderburn did not invite his son Robert Wedderburn into his house at Inveresk Lodge in 1795. However, in 2003 Lord Bill Wedderburn, the distinguished scholar, and his wife Lady Frances Wedderburn and I were allowed inside the Lodge. Time and endeavour enabled us to complete what Robert Wedderburn had intended to do in 1795. Lord (Professor) Wedderburn is a proud descendant of the slave Robert Wedderburn. Both he and Frances came back to Inveresk Lodge in 2007, to participate in the commemoration of the 200th anniversary of the Abolition of the British Slave Trade. *The Robert Wedderburn Walk* was staged by a large diverse group of people to honour and remember the pilgrimage made by Robert Wedderburn in 1795 (article 17).

~ Biography ~

THE AUTHOR

Geoff Henry Palmer is Professor of Grain Science at a University near Edinburgh and has received various awards for his research and community work. Recently he not only received a distinguished research award as a grain scientist from the American Society of Brewing Chemists, he was also awarded the Sir William Y. Darling bequest from The Edinburgh City Council for his work in "race relations", the OBE (Order of the British Empire) for his research contribution to grain science and the "Black Champion" award for notable contribution to the community in 2002, 2003 and 2004 respectively. He regards this narrative as an attempt to show the terrible consequences of slavery, ignorance and prejudice. Examples of his work on these topics are presented in newspaper articles referenced and reproduced below.

These were written to inform our education and justice systems of some of the difficulties Black-British children face in this society. Despite a large 'race relations industry' many of these problems remain…maybe new approaches are required to remove the erroneous perception that black people have not and do not contribute to the good image and wealth of the country. His recently published short story, 'Mr White and the Ravens' (ISBN: 0-9549519-1-3), Henry Publishing, Scotland, is a new or alternative approach at showing the social damage that can be caused by imperialistic ideology based on ignorance and prejudice (articles 13, 14, 19).

Professor Palmer maintains that the anomalous word 'race' is judgemental, divisive, scientifically meaningless and re-inforces prejudice. Its origins and meaning are uncertain. It is divisive and should, in future, be abolished and never be applied to human beings. Surely, identical hearts are more important than differences in skin colour. However, in this narrative, it is used as expected. In terms of logic, it is nonsense to refer to 'races of people' and retain the concept of Human race. Instead of using the phrase 'race relations', we should concentrate our efforts on improving Human relations. In contrast to the word race, the word Human provides a more accurate description of our equality as people. That a large group of white teachers, to whom Professor Palmer was lecturing, declined to define the word race suggests that they were either ignorant of the word or afraid of its politics...no one should be put in such a position in any society.

Professor Palmer believes that 'equal opportunity' is a pointless concept if people do not have the means to realise opportunities. Education should be used to ensure and secure rights. However, if education fails the law cannot afford to fail. He hopes that others, who work in this area, will do all they can to educate those who would deny the rights of other human beings. Finally the author thanks many people for support: Family, friends, Craig Nicol for design and print input, the Jamaican Archive and those who sent the surprising but encouraging responses to the publication, 'Mr White and the Ravens'. Professor Palmer's optimism regarding human affinity is derived from the view that politically, it has always been very destructive to keep people apart anywhere in the world.

ARTICLES:

1. 'Where Children are Still Seen and Not Heard' (page 110) ,
The Times Educational Supplement, 20.3.1970

2. 'No Kill Nobody but a Policeman',
The Times Educational Supplement, 16.10.1970

3. 'Handsworth: Caribbean Black Country' (page 115),
*The Times Educational Supplement, 16.6.1972 (**Postscript** 2004)*

4. 'Breaking Away for the Black Stereotype',
Geoff Palmer speaking to Colleen Williams
The Weekly Gleaner, 15.8.1986

5. 'Multicultural Education',
Church of Scotland report to the General Assembly:
Committee on Education Report to Board of Education
(response to Swann's "Education for All") Chaired by G.H.Palmer,
Edinburgh, 1990

6. 'Food for Thought in a Multicultural Britain' (page 126),
Sunday Express, 25.6.2000

7. 'Brewing up a Storm',
Geoff Palmer speaking to Kenneth Taylor
The Voice, 17 and 24.12.2001

8. 'Punished for being Jamaican'...new Visa Regime (page 130),
The Edinburgh Evening News, 25.1.2003

9. 'Education Race and Citizenship' (page 135)
School of the Divinity, Centre for Theology and Public Issues
Edinburgh University, 2004

10. Robert Wedderburn:
'Disowned by his Father...for the Colour of His Skin',
Geoff Palmer speaking to Sandra Dick
Edinburgh Evening News, 9.6.2003

11. 'Go Back and Grow Bananas',
Geoff Palmer speaking to Olga Wojtas
Times Higher Educational Supplement, 15.8.2003

12. 'The Race to Open Our Borders and Our Minds'
Geoff Palmer speaking to Tom Lynch,
The Sunday Times, 29.4.2004

13. 'My Colour Is Me'
(Based on article, Freedom Colour Prejudice (page 140)
Geoff Palmer
Black Information Link, website, 26.2.2007

14. 'The Registrar-General and the Black and White Question
in Scotland'
Geoff Palmer
The Herald, 20.3.2007

15. 'Still Fighting for Freedom'
Geoff Palmer speaking to Cassandra Jardine,
The Daily Telegraph, 22.3.2007

16. 'Walkers to Remember Strides Taken by Anti-slavery Activist'
(page 143) Geoff Palmer speaking to Adrian Mather,
Edinburgh Evening News, 23.4.2007

17. 'The 200th year Commemoration of the Abolition of the British Slave Trade in the West Indies: 1807-2007' (page 143) Robert Wedderburn Freedom Walk: From Musselburgh High Street to Inveresk Lodge. Geoff Palmer:
Written for the National Trust for Scotland, 2007

18. 'Geoff Palmer' Interviewed by Gavin D Smith
Scotch Whisky Review, Spring, 2007

19. 'Wicked Commerce'
Geoff Palmer
Black London Magazine, Bicentennial Edition, April, 2007.

TELEVISION CONTRIBUTION:

BBC 2: Andrew Watson, the 19th Century black football captain of Scotland, 2003.

BBC 2: 'The Scottish Empire', *Programme 2 (West Indian Slavery), Wark Clements Production, 2004.*

BBC: *www.bbc.co.uk/scotland/education/hist/abolition, September, 2007.*

For who would bear the whips and scorns of time,

The oppressor's wrong, the proud man's contumely,

The pangs of dispriz'd love, the law's delay,

The insolence of office...

Shakespeare

Whatever mitigates the woes or increases the happiness of others,

this is my criterion of goodness; and whatever injures society at

large or any individual in it, this is my measure of iniquity...

Burns

But someday, somebody'll

stand up and talk about me

and write about me

black and beautiful

and sing about me

and put on plays about me!

I reckon it'll be

me myself!

Yes, it'll be me.

Hughes

834   Montego-Bay, Dec 14, 1790.

FOR SALE,

On Thursday the 23d instant,

439 Prime, Healthy, Young, EBOE

NEGROES,

Imported in the Ship

BROTHERS,

Captain JOSEPH WITHERS,
From BONNY.

James Wedderburn & Co.

Preface To Slavery

BRITISH CHATTEL SLAVERY: THE ABOLITION OF
THE BRITISH SLAVE TRADE (1807)

We are the descendants of black Chattel slaves that were giants.
They gave us their lives to live with honour.

During the commemoration of the 200th anniversary of the abolition of the British slave trade it has been stated, in various quarters, that Chattel slavery, to which the slaves of the West Indies were subjected, is similar to human trafficking, indentured labour or even Clearance of the Scottish Highlands (1746). This argument of denial has been used to dilute the brutal slavery to which our ancestors were subjected for over three hundred years. Some people have refused to take part in the commemoration because, although they readily glorify the good deeds of their ancestors, they are slow to acknowledge the crimes they committed. Curiously, these are the people who want us to "learn" British history. Is Chattel slavery not British history?

The British (Barbados) Chattel Slave Code (1661), adopted as the Slave Code in America, was used to great effect by British slave masters: It required by law that, all slaves should be clothed. However, it also denied slaves basic human rights guaranteed under British law such as the right to life. It allowed slave owners to do entirely as they wished to their slaves, including mutilating them and burning them alive, without fear of reprisal. This also meant that the children of slaves belonged to slave masters and they were sold by them. White slave masters often freed their mixed race children but also had the right to sell them. The British Slave Code meant that *a slave master could legally kill his slave.* If you have no human rights, only then can you be called a Chattel slave. Therefore, when Luke Collingwood, Captain of the British slave ship the Zong, threw his slaves overboard and drowned them in 1781, to gain the insurance, he was tried but found not guilty of murder. He had not broken British slave laws; the judge ruled that the slaves Collingwood had killed were Chattel, not human beings. Collingwood was therefore found not guilty of murder. Is this equivalent to the injustices of trafficking ("modern slavery"), which is not legal? To compare trafficking to Chattel slavery is an insult to the millions of black people that died as British slaves. There can be no religious, biological, philosophical or moral excuse for the unacceptable legal contrivance at Collingwood's trial. Human beings are human beings not animals: no-one could have failed to recognise this.

It is worrying that the commemorations will pass and the horror of Chattel slavery will not be understood because many of the books, articles and official documents do not mention the word Chattel thereby understating the brutality of New World slavery. After giving a lecture to children on Chattel slavery and illustrating it with the case of the *Zong* a teenager in the audience said, "I can understand why the captain threw the sick slaves overboard, but it was a waste that he drowned the healthy slaves too." If this is the nature of our moral education in schools, the unthinking response of those who would deny British slavery is understandable. At the end of another lecture, a Minister of the Church said that although he was familiar with African history he was unaware of Scotland's involvement in British slavery. In a letter, another Minister regarded the documented life of Robert Wedderburn as a "tale" and objected to people knowing that his town had an association with slavery. He also remarked that the images of slavery were too upsetting for the town's children to see...but in an unprincipled way failed to consider the children of slaves who had to watch the brutality. Nevertheless, to show he was a man of God and mercy he added in his letter that he would give some pulpit time to human trafficking ("modern slavery"). Why? Is it because "modern slavery" carries no 'sins' to which he can be connected? Such is the poor regard for our section of British history that the truth about its slavery can be dismissed cynically as a...bad historical tale. Indeed, when I stated to a Professor from Hull University that he should have used his Rowntree grant money to compare British Chattel Slavery with "modern slavery" rather than compare "British Slavery with "modern slavery", he promised clarification but failed to respond. He was fully aware that his proposal, that "British Slavery" was the same as "modern slavery", was a lie to promote the trafficking campaign. Trafficking is wrong but for an academic to misrepresent the meaning of Chattel slavery is disgraceful.

A reprehensible tactic of racists is to frustrate justice for others by saying, "Others suffered too..." It is wrong to link one evil with another because doing so diminishes both evils. Each evil requires separate attention. Deception and ignorance that masquerade as balance or compassion is malicious and destructive. I have the conscience to respect the history of others...what kind of conscience must racists have to deny the history and identity of other people?

Before progressing with this narrative on British slavery, it is regrettable that in the year of remembering the holocaust of British Chattel slavery in the West Indies, civil servants in Scotland, England and Wales have initiated a process to abolish the categories, black and white from census forms. The final objective is to remove black and white from all official documents. The removal of white is a deceptive palliative because white people are not abused because of their colour and their needs are the best met in our diverse society. In contrast, the removal of black will increase racial abuse of black people and eliminate the means by which colour prejudice is monitored. The excuses given for this untimely attempt to remove the identity of black people are that a small group of Africans, not "Africans in Scotland" as reported, find the category black insulting and, to white people, black means "power". Both reasons are presented without valid scientific evidence. However, I would have thought that "white" portrays more power than "black" in our society.

In many ways the actions of these civil servants are prejudicial and are likely to damage race relations. I stated these views in an article to the Black Information Link and in a letter to The (Glasgow) Herald newspaper (see articles 13 and 14). I regarded it as astonishing that, in the year of the commemoration of the abolition of the slave trade the black identity of the descendants of British slavery is being questioned without their consent. This unequal action of our civil servants merges into institutional racism. It is also being proposed that black people should be called "Africans" and white people should be called "Europeans". That such dangerous nonsense could be distributed by civil servants without government approval is frightening. Somehow, black West Indian identity will be abolished, so will white African identity...

The vast majority of Africans, West Indians whom I know are not ashamed of their black colour and were not, like myself, consulted regarding the concept of abolishing black and white. The tampering with colour identities of black and white people is intended to please a small group of Africans...this excuse defies understanding and a more serious explanation must be given for the cost incurred and the damage done, especially to the dignity of black people. The indecent haste with which this was done should be questioned because such haste has never been applied to addressing the social, educational or medical needs of black people.

The negative image created about black people caused them to be enslaved. It took many great black people such as Garvey, Sengor, Hughes, Malcolm X, King, Rosa Parks, Baldwin, Kenyatta, Nkrumah, Biko and Mandela to make black dignified and beautiful again. Human beings have the right to define their own identities. My identity is black Jamaican and I have the genetic and legal right to live in Scotland and in any other part of Britain. Many West Indians can claim Scottish heritage...they already have the family names. My black lineage stems from the New World (Jamaican) slavery of my ancestors. I have no legal right to live in Africa but I am proud of my historical links with Africa. All human beings should be proud of their association with Africa... because we all came from Africa. Notwithstanding, it still remains beyond all forms of reason to understand why a band of white civil servants would want black people of independent West Indian nations to call themselves Africans. I cannot see why anyone should ask a Kenyan or Nigerian to become a Jamaican or a Guyanese. No black person will sign or barter away the lineage and freedom of his or her black identity (Interestingly, The British Council of Muslims which is an organisation of diverse people has stated that the census categories, black and white, should be retained). Now, it is evident that the murderous journey, from the 15th century introduction of black Chattel slavery, to its legal abolition in the 19th century, is a historical journey we should all know because the consequences of this brutal slavery are still with us today.

When did black slavery begin? In 1444 the Portuguese took black people from Africa and forced them to work in Portugal. In 1455, the Pope ruled that "infidel people" should be "reduced to servitude". In 1456 the Portuguese took the Cape Verde islands and introduced slaves to plant sugar cane and make sugar. Columbus's discovery of the New World in 1492 gave Spain a very large colonial Empire to grow cane and other valuable crops. Sugar, rum, coffee, spices and cotton soon became part of the rich life-style of Europe...and for hundreds of years were the objects of bitter wars. The British, French, Spanish, Dutch, Danish and Portuguese fought each other at sea for pieces of the New World on which they could force black slaves to produce their goods. In 1553, Sir William Cecil, the English politician, stated that effective occupation was the determinant of sovereignty. Therefore the British, like other European nations, started to acquire, by conquest or discovery, colonies in the New World.

By 1553, the European Chattel slave industry was in place. In 1562 John Hawkins started the British slave trade business with the blessings of his Queen, Elizabeth I. The ingredients of this slave industry were land, black slaves, unpaid labour and merciless slave masters, in a hurry to be rich. The profit was money, as much as possible, in the shortest possible time. Nothing can stop greed with a gun. The most powerful nations in the world, Britain, France, Spain, Portugal, and the Dutch controlled half a world of slaves that was 5,000 miles away in the West Indies. Never in the history of the world were so many naval wars fought for one area of the world. The British Navy was at its most powerful and Naval Captains such as Benbow, Rodney, Nelson, Howe, Hood, Bligh, Duckworth, Wallis, Vincent and others are now part of the elite history of the British Navy because they protected the British Slave Empire in the New World. At the end of the seven years war in 1763, Britain took the slave colonies it wanted...it kept and took those best suited to grow sugar and coffee. As part of the tradition of defending British interests in the West Indies, Horatio Nelson honed his fighting skills in the West Indies. His many duties in the West Indies resulted in his marriage being held in Barbados where he was stationed. During slavery Britain lost more men fighting in the West Indies than it lost fighting in Europe over the same period. Chattel slavery was important to the British economy and no attempt to abolish it before it had run its course would have been tolerated by the British Parliament. That is why British slavery in the New World lasted nearly 300 years...the abolition movements came at the end of this very long silence of injustice.

The economic importance of British slavery was so well established that even a radical poet such as Robert Burns thanked Admiral Rodney for defending Jamaica from the French and the Spanish at the Battle of the Saints (also called, The Battle of the Glorious 12th of April) in 1782. This was the beating in the West Indies that "softened up" the French, for Lord Nelson to defeat at Trafalgar in 1805. Jamaica had to be defended. At that period Jamaica was the most important sugar producing country in the British Empire. It was also the main destination of British (mainly English and Scottish) fortune hunters. Although poorly educated, part of my training in Britishness in secondary school in Jamaica, was to repeat Admiral Benbow's gallantry and Rodney's victory. I have met only one white British person who knew of Rodney's victory or its importance in British history. For winning this pivotal battle against France and Spain, Rodney was elevated to the Peerage and given a pension of about £2,000,000, at today's money value. Therefore, when we commemorate the abolition of the slave trade, it should not be forgotten that it took nearly three hundred years for the British Parliament to be told, collectively, that its slavery of black people was inhuman and wrong. Before 1782, The Church and the Nation benefited in silence as many millions of slaves suffered and died. The Church of England owned slaves and branded SOCIETY on their chests, the Church of Scotland did not petition for abolition and excluded slaves from its church services in Jamaica during slavery. The other churches spoke to slaves such as Sam Sharpe (1831) whose Christianity assisted his determination to fight for freedom. Sharpe was a Baptist, so were Bogle and Gordon. The Baptist Church came to Jamaica in 1814. In the face of injustice, silence is the great evil.

The New World slave plantation system was based on the economic premise that large quantities of cultivatable land that produced desirable products, with free labour, would be extremely profitable. First it was thought that the native Indians or white indentured labourers would provide free or cheap labour respectively. This was not successful. The slaving practice of the Portuguese was adopted. Based on prejudice alone, it was decided that black slaves from Africa would produce more work in the inhospitable conditions of New World Plantations. Indentured labourers had agreements which limited their working hours and time. They were also paid.

Killing them or their children was a crime. The "bonus" of using black slaves was that they would not be paid and they could be worked to death.

There have been numerous academic arguments that paid work is more profitable than "slave" labour. Even if working practice is inefficient, a large free source of forced labour is infinitely more profitable than any other kind of labour. Even Adam Smith (1723 – 1790), the father of capitalism, admitted that this concept was correct. He stated that: *The profits of a sugar plantation in any of our West Indian colonies are generally much greater than those from any other civilisation known either in Europe or America.* The "free" slave labour to which Smith also refers in some of his writings pertains to white "slave by name" labour ...not Chattel slavery. Chattel slavery embodied forced wage-free labour. This practice made British slavery in the West Indies, the most profitable evil the world has known. Charles Davenant (1656 – 1714) the English economist said that, every white person from the British Islands in the West Indies brought in £10 (£1,000 at today's value) clear annual profit to England; twenty times as much as a similar person in the Home Counties of England. William Pitt (1759 – 1806), the British Prime Minister, asserted in 1798 that, the annual income from the West Indian plantations was £4 million (about £400,000,000 at today's value) compared with £1 million (about £100,000,000) from the rest of the world. Nearly two-thirds of this (£400,000,000) came from Jamaica alone.

To secure an efficient supply of slaves for the production of sugar, cotton, coffee, spices and rum an efficient supply of slaves was required. John Hawkins, a merchant/adventurer, with the encouragement of Elizabeth 1, started the British slave trade by capturing black slaves in Africa and selling them in the New World, in 1562. Many more merchants/adventurers joined the trade. To make the trade more profitable, The Royal African Company was set up in 1660 by the Royal Stuart family and reformed in 1672. It was headed by the brother of Charles II...James II. Its business purpose was to purchase or capture "Negro" slaves to supply the plantations of the New World. A slave bought from an African trader for £2 could be sold for £60 into slavery. The efficiency in securing and transporting slaves was increased after the dissolution of the Royal African Company in 1698. This new free trade transported over 2 million slaves between 1680 and 1786.

Between 1700 and 1800, there were about 11,000 slave-ship sailings from London, Bristol and Liverpool. Sailings from Scotland increased many fold over this period. Act 4 of The Union of the Scottish and English Parliaments gave the Scots permission to enter the profitable English slave market which took Scotland out of poverty. After the signing of the Political Acts of the Union, Scots not only entered West Indian slavery, they also established business interest in Chesapeake in Virginia, America. By 1740 the tobacco trade in Chesapeake was dominated by Glasgow tobacco merchants. They became very rich trading tobacco grown by slaves. Many were millionaires and invested money in the development of Glasgow. Some of Glasgow's streets still bear their surnames: Buchanan, Ingram and Glasford. Grand constructions such as Virginia Buildings and William Cunninghame's house, which is the exquisite part of the Gallery of Modern Art, were both built with money gained from slavery. As Tobacco lords, Buchanan, Ingram, Glasford and Cunninghame, like other Tobacco lords, exuded great power in Glasgow. In contrast to the Tobacco lords, James Ewing (1775-1853) was a Sugar baron (in his time, the best known public figure in Glasgow). He inherited large sugar plantations in Jamaica and initiated the building of the Glasgow Necropolis (1828) and is buried there, next to the giant statue of John Knox.

The fortunes of the Tobacco lords declined rapidly at the beginning of the American Revolution in 1775. The Americans started to manage their own tobacco trade. Tobacco lords such as Cunninghame shifted from tobacco to sugar. He had a large sugar plantation in Jamaica which was managed by the Wedderburns, suggesting that exploitation of the slaves was a complex partnership business of money-making and forging new family connections. If Virginia was the focus of British slave grown tobacco, the West Indies was the focus of slave grown sugar and coffee and the Scots were in the West Indies in large numbers. By 1807 there were about 20,000 white people in Jamaica, about half of these were Scots and about one-third of the slave plantations were owned by Scots.

At the end of slavery in 1834, the slave masters, who retained their land, were given free, so-called "Apprentice Scheme" slave labour for four years. Also, they were given over £2 billion (at today's value) by the British government to "free" their slaves. The slaves were given nothing. The parasitic existence of the slave masters continued even after slavery was finally abolished in 1838, with the ending of the "Apprenticeship Scheme". This was the cause of the great loss of life in the Morant Bay Rebellion of Bogle and Gordon, in Jamaica, in 1865 which ended the exploitation of the decendants of slaves in Jamaica. Bogle, Gordon and many other Jamaicans were hanged. The power of the slave masters was removed finally when Jamaica and the other slave colonies became Crown Colonies, ruled directly from Britain. Slavery in Jamaica did not really end until the Morant Bay rebellion in 1865. Not one of the supportive voices from the anti-slavery movement was heard when Thomas Carlyle (1867) praised Governor Eyre for hanging Jamaicans that rebelled at Morant Bay in 1865. Carlyle berated black people as "Niggers" and "Quashes". He bemoaned the loss of the free labour which sustained British slavery... he and others could not accept that the parasitic "free meal" of British slavery was over. War-like rebellions were the only way black people could make the British government understand that slavery was wrong and, in time, would be unworkable.

In the greatest forced mass-transportation of people the world has known, about 20 million black Africans were transported, like animals, from the West Coast of Africa as slaves and about 10 million survived to work on the plantations. This transportation was part of a *Triangular Trade*. Slave ships sailed from British ports such as Bristol, Liverpool, London and sometimes Glasgow. On the West Coast of Africa slaves were packed onto the decks of ships, like sardines in a tin. These ships then sailed "the middle passage" across the Atlantic to the plantations of the New World. Voyages could last longer than a month. Sick or dead slaves were thrown overboard. Some slaves dismayed by this mysterious degradation fought to be free, others drowned themselves. Beatings were brutal...all this cruelty was within the laws of British Chattel slavery. Slaves were washed, greased and sold on arrival or sold-on to other destinations. Jamaica was not only a port for the sale of slaves; it was also a staging post for the distribution of slaves to other countries in the New World. Between 1700 and 1786, about 610, 000 slaves were transported to Jamaica. New slaves were subjected to "seasoning periods" of ill treatment, to condition them to work as dictated. The length of the daylight hours of the day determined the length of the working day of a slave. *The average working life of a slave was less than five years.* The third leg of the trade was from the slave colonies, back to Britain. The ships were laden with the produce of the plantations. A two-way trade also occurred. Ships sailed from Bristol, Liverpool, London, Glasgow, Greenock and Leith to the West Indies with supplies and white immigrants. They then returned to these ports with the produce of slavery.

The short working life of a Chattel slave mattered little to the slave owners. The slave trade made it easy to replace slaves. However, by abolition the slave islands were very well stocked with slaves. On the small island of Jamaica, there were, at the time, about 300,000 slaves. The slave masters had solid support in the British Parliament and in their local Assemblies because of their wealth. Without the vote, petitions helped to bring matters of concern to the Government. In addition to petitions and the great support from Quakers (1783) the members of the Society for the Abolition of the Slave Trade (1787) such as Granville Sharp, Thomas Clarkson, James Ramsay, William Dickson, Zachary Macaulay, James Stephen and Henry Broughton persuaded William Wilberforce to pursue the abolition campaign in Parliament.

Wilberforce's Parliamentary bill to abolish the slave trade was supported by a large number of petitions from Scotland and England but the bill was rejected at least seven times from 1791 before it passed into an Act in 1807. Black (non-white) activists such as Jamaican born, Robert Wedderburn (1762 - 1835) and African born Olaudah Equiano (1745 – 1797) also played an active part in securing abolition of the slave trade. Wedderburn was relentless in his attack on those who enslaved his family and his people in the West Indies. Robert Wedderburn's father, James Wedderburn, was a wealthy Scottish slave master who made his money in, Westmoreland, Jamaica. Robert's mother was a black slave, called Rosanna. James Wedderburn rejected his black son. The distinguished Professor and economist, Lord Bill Wedderburn, QC, is a proud descendant of Robert Wedderburn. Bill Wedderburn earned his awards and is fiercely proud of his slave ancestor.

We are descended from great men like Robert Wedderburn and the leaders of our slave rebellions. It is baffling that Scots like James Wedderburn and his family who suffered after losing the war at Culloden in 1745, could go to Jamaica and be so barbaric to black slaves in pursuit of money, is difficult to explain. Was it misplaced revenge, greed or the desire to recover what they had lost: pride, power and status? The evil mix of British slavery is complex and requires detailed study to unravel the diabolical nature of this event...an event, and its consequences, that still defy understanding. A small grant here and small grant there will not produce anything of scientific value. At its simplest, one may ask: *How could "enlightened people" allow Chattel slavery to go on for so long?* Those who think we should forget this slavery are under the illusion that we understand the potential of human beings to commit evil.

The abolition of the slave trade increased the price of slaves. Despite the efforts of the British Navy to stop the trade in slaves, slave traders still traded with Cuba and Brazil. American slavery did not end until 1865 and it continued to sell its surplus slaves. To counter the effects of the abolition of the slave trade, letters from slave masters (see page 46) often lamented the "waste" of feeding slaves incapable of doing profitable work and outlined that "breeding of slaves" was being tried to offset potential labour shortages that could occur because of the abolition of the British slave trade. Had British slavery been abolished totally in 1807, instead of 31 years later in 1838, the barbaric practice of trying to "breed" people would not have been enacted against black British slaves. Evil must be stopped with one debilitating blow or else it will grow again and spread as it did for 31 years after the abolition of the slave trade.

Religious and political justifications for slavery were provided by many people but probably the most devastating justification for the enslavement of black people came from respected philosopher David Hume in 1753. He stated, without reservation, that black people were inferior to white people...black people could imitate white people, not equal them. It is beyond belief that Hume, one of the great thinkers of the Enlightenment, could not see that differences in life-style did not reflect differences in intelligence. Because of his vast reputation as a thinker, Hume's bad reasoning was used by slave masters as scientific justification for the enslavement of black people. In Hume's time, slavery could not be criticised because of the power of the merchants...maybe Hume was concerned with his own self-interest when he contrived his racist conclusions.

Unfortunately, Hume's racist views are still at the root of racist thinking today. To have the British Parliament, rich merchants, political power and the whips and scorns of slave masters against you as a slave is beyond our comprehension. Yet, the slaves survived to be our ancestors. Through us, these slaves will live and their story will no longer be denied by mindless people, *as "a tale of bad history"*.

The British Parliament was reluctant to abolish the lucrative trade in human beings. Many MPs colluded for years to prolong slavery...many Scottish MPs never voted for the abolition process. Abolition of the slave trade, before the abolition of total slavery, was the rotten compromise the abolitionists and Wilberforce accepted because of the intransigence of powerful government ministers such as, the Scot, Henry Dundas...rewarded later, with a very tall statue in St Andrews square in Edinburgh and the title of Lord Melville, for protecting British interests during slavery. He had family connections with the slave master, James Wedderburn. His political approach was simple. Slavery was awful but it was an essential part of the British economy and had to be prolonged. He knew that this cynical concept of self-interest could not be challenged in the short term. In the late 1700s and early 1800s, abolitionists such as William Dickson (a Scot) organised petitions against slavery. However, those who opposed slavery were out of step with the general view that slavery was in Britain's interest. Rev

James Lapsley of Campsie in Scotland was so convinced of this that he ensured that those who opposed slavery were prosecuted. However, neither petitions nor prayer could have swayed Dundas away from his political plans for prolonging slavery for as long as possible. He was the protector of rich slave-owning merchants and they supported him.

William Pitt, the Prime Minister, although acknowledged as one of the most gifted of British politicians, was powerless, compared to Dundas, with regard the abolition of slavery. Pitt regarded his greatest failure, before he died in 1806, as not being able to abolish British slavery. At that time, Dundas was in charge of the British Navy and was known as the uncrowned king of Scotland. Like Napoleon, he tried to stop Toussaint L'Ouverture's slave rebellions in Haiti that led to Haiti's independence in 1804. He failed and many British servicemen died. However, at home, he made it clear to Wilberforce that the condition for Parliament passing the Slave Trade Act was...that slavery should be "gradually abolished", which meant: *delayed abolition of slavery.* Dundas's deception became law and British slavery went on for another 31 years. Wilberforce and his abolitionist supporters accepted this rotten compromise which led to the contemptible practice of promoting the breeding of slaves (see letter, pages 46-48). Granville Sharp and later Clarkson regretted making this compromise but the power of Dundas, through Parliament, won the day, and the abolition of the slave trade was separated from the abolition of slavery. Amid the "praises" for abolitionists lurks the murderous tragedy of a slavery that should have been abolished at once, rather than in slow stages to secure the best profit.

The profits from slavery were so important to British interests that slavery was allowed to continue for another 27 years, after the abolition of the trade in 1807. After the abolition of slavery in 1834, there were another 4 years of delay, known as the iniquitous "Apprenticeship System" in which free slaves had to work for their old masters without a wage under a "milder" slavery. In this "milder" slavery, marriage would be allowed if sanctioned by the slave master. Women were to be flogged in private, instead of in public. Maximum lashes would be 39... *such were the perverted principles of The Enlightenment that kept the slave captive.*

Percival (1762-1812) was a powerful politician during the abolition process. It is not often stated that he helped Wilberforce to secure the Slave Trade Abolition Act in 1807. It is not well known that he was assassinated by a disaffected merchant in Parliament...the only British Prime Minister to be assassinated. Another person that supported Wilberforce was John Newton, the converted slaveship captain who wrote the Hymns: *Amazing Grace* and *How Sweet the Name of Jesus Sounds.* In some ways John Newton's life (1725-1807) mirrored the ambiguity of the Church during slavery. Some Churches branded their slaves; others did not petition for abolition, others excluded slaves from worship while others were late in supporting the abolition process. However, it is important to mention that the fighting spirit of the slaves increased with Christianity, as the slave masters had feared. Therefore, before Samuel Sharpe was hanged in Jamaica, in 1832, for leading the Christmas rebellion, he made his position as a Christian clear. He declared that the only master he would serve was not the one that owned him on the plantations but the one that owned him in heaven. Reverend Knibb, a Baptist Minister in Jamaica, worked valiantly to end slavery. On his arrival in Jamaica from Britain in 1823 he said, *I have reached the land of sin, disease and death.* And before Knibb, Dr Johnson (died 1784) described Jamaica as, *a place of great wealth, a den of tyrants and a dungeon of slaves.* The work of other abolitionists such as Thomas Buxton, Andrew Thomson and Joseph Sturge complemented the work of Knibb which encouraged the British Parliament and the Colonial Assemblies to end slavery in 1838. Knibb died in Jamaica and is buried in his Church in Jamaica.

To the slave master, politician and merchant, slavery was a "natural" pursuit of "self interest". The song, *Rule Britannia* was written by the Scot, James Thompson, in 1740. It puts so called European Enlightenment into its true context of shameful arrogance and interest in self that mocks: We enslave others, they don't enslave us. In addition, the great hypocrisy of British justice during slavery is summarised in the self-congratulating court cases of the British slaves, Somerset and Joseph Knight. Somerset was set free by Lord Mansfield in London in 1772. Joseph Knight was set free in Scotland in 1778.

These judgements made it clear that whilst slavery was not permitted in England and Scotland, it was permitted in the colonies of the West Indies where English and Scottish people ran rampant as slavers. This "two-faced" justice exemplified the kind of hypocrisy that kept the disease of slavery alive for so long and made it seem acceptable to white young men such as the poet Robert Burns (died 1796) who bought his ticket in 1786 to sail to Jamaica to become, in his own words, a "Negro driver". Thankfully, Burns did not sail. In his poem about "honest poverty", he wrote: *That man to man the world over/Shall brothers be...* However, the young white men that sailed to the West Indies became "Whippers-in" of slaves according to the poet Coleridge (died 1834). This was their way of achieving a large fortune quickly. Where was the brotherly love then? It certainly was not on the slave plantations. However, out of the evil of slavery has come, not only bad money but good things such as new nations of people, new pride in colour and self, new forms of music such as Blues, Jazz and popular music such as Rap and Reggae. The hymn *Amazing Grace* which was written by the ex-slaveship captain John Newton is also a legacy of slavery; so is *Ae Fond Kiss*, by Burns. He wrote it to bid his lady friend, Clarinda (Mrs MacLehose) goodbye as she sailed from Greenock in 1791 to meet her husband who was a slave master in Jamaica. She informed Burns on her return to Scotland that her husband told her to return to Edinburgh alone because he was quite happy with his, *Ebony (slave) woman and mahogany children.*

Despite the constraints of a vicious slavery, the slaves fought for their freedom and the threat of a Haiti-type rebellion, where independence was granted by the French in 1804, was a constant worry to British politicians and slave masters. Over a period of one hundred years there was at least one dangerous slave rebellion in Jamaica every ten years in which both white slave masters and slaves died. Similar rebellions also occurred in other slave colonies. The maroons (black slaves of captured Spanish territories) were involved in some of these rebellions. In Jamaica they signed treaties with the British that freed them from working as slaves. The defiance and executions of great patriots such as Bussa (1816), Gladstone (1823) and Sharpe (1832) occurred after the abolition of the slave trade but sent a serious message to the British Parliament that total abolition would have to be given because the killings would not stop. As the Baptist Christian, Samuel Sharpe, said at his hanging in Jamaica in 1832: *I would rather die upon yonder gallows than live in slavery.*

The role of the British Navy in protecting British colonies from the French was expensive in life and money. Some British women signed petitions to abolish slavery because of the large numbers of sailors that were dying in the seemingly continuous battles with the French and Spanish. The industrial revolution in the 1830s was throwing up new problems of social unrest at home. The control of Britain's slave business, 5,000 miles away, was also problematic. Sugar was cheap in Cuba and Britain wanted to "take advantage" of this source of slave-produced sugar. Despite British Naval patrols after the abolition of the slave trade, slaves were still being transported to Brazil and Cuba. In general, mindful of the successful rebellion in Haiti by the slaves, British Chattel slavery was becoming dangerous, impractical and indecent. Full abolition was inevitable. The resistance of the slaves, against the most powerful country in the world, and their role in securing abolition should be given proper recognition. Many acts of slave defiance are mentioned among the terrible events recorded by the Jamaican slave master, Thistlewood, in his diary of 1750 to 1786. This diary is a dispassionate, personal catalogue of legal brutality and rape. In it, Thistlewood quotes a slave as saying: *If this is life then let me die.* This was a slavery that was worse than death. With a black lineage which started with Giants of black British rebellions such as Tacky, Sharpe, Bussa, Gladstone, Gordon and Bogle...why should I not fight to keep my black-slave identity. With such a defiant and distinguished history of survival why should I look elsewhere for an identity? As I said in one of my articles, my colour is me and nothing will change my position on identity. Each person has a right to choose his or her identity.

The history of British slavery should be taught routinely so that people can make up their own minds regarding the contribution West Indian people have made to the development of Britain. Such knowledge will help to remove those areas of ignorance which produce racism.

The amount of money made from British West Indian slavery is impossible to estimate. A price cannot be put on suffering. Horace Walpole (1750), the British Member of Parliament, said that although Chattel slavery, *Chills one's blood,* the economy of Britain depended on the money made from this trade. Slave merchants and slave masters such as Scotsmen: John Gladstone (the father of William Gladstone, the British Prime Minister), Archibald Grant. James Ewing, William Cunninghame, Richard Oswald, and James Wedderburn became multi-millionaires. For example, when John Gladstone died he left about £65 million (today's value). James Ewing's estate was worth about £22 million (today's value). English slavers such as, William Beckford and Henry Lascelle were even richer. William Beckford (1760-1844) owned 22,000 acres of slave plantations in Jamaica and was, at one time, the richest man in Europe...and one of the richest in the world. He was Lord Mayor of London and is reputed to have hired Mozart to give his son piano lessons. Slave money helped these families to buy their way into Parliament and the aristocracy and to build grand monuments, not in slave fields, but in various parts of Britain.

Powerful slave families such as the Lascelles and the Wedderburns had many slave plantations. The Lascelles had slave plantations in Barbados and Jamaica. They built, Harewood House in Yorkshire... one of the grandest stately homes in Britain. The present Lord Harewood is a Lascelle and has family links to the Royal Family through his late mother, HRH Princess Mary. James Wedderburn's father was hanged after the battle of Colluden of 1745. He and his brother went to Jamaica in 1746 and became slave masters.

The Wedderburn family of uncles and nephews built a "slave empire" in Westmoreland in Jamaica. The family eventually owned the following estates: Jerusalem, Retreat, Moreland, Paradise, Mount Edgecombe, Clenisia, Spring Garden, Baulk, Blue Castle and Blackheath. They also managed estates for absentee landlords such as Cunninghame who owned a 3,500 acre estate called Grandvale. After returning to Inveresk in Scotland in 1773 James Wedderburn bought a Lodge and married the daughter and heir of the last Lord Colvile. His daughter (Jean) married Lord Selkirk who owned a substantial part of Manitoba (which included the Winnipeg area), Canada. One of his sons became Lord Advocate. Another son, Andrew Wedderburn-Colvile, the one who stated that his black slave-born half-brother, Robert Wedderburn, did not count as family, managed his father's slave business in Jamaica while acting as Chairman of the West India Docks in London. He dropped the name Wedderburn and used Colvile. He then became a Governor of the Hudson Bay Company and married Lord Auckland's daughter. Their son, Eden, also became a Governor of the Hudson Bay Company. Lord Auckland was a good friend of the Prime Minister, Lord Grenville. Grenville was Prime Minister when the slave trade was abolished in 1807. Andrew Wedderburn-Colvile was the most powerful and celebrated Governor of the Hudson Bay Company and many places in Canada and the United States are named after him...as Colvile.

I do not know how the black Jamaican descendants of James Wedderburn live in Jamaica but I am sure they are less well placed than his white descendants.They were not born with blood-stained silver spoons of slavery in their mouths. The present Lord Dundee is a descendant of James Wedderburn. In passing, James Wedderburn's brother, John Wedderburn had a daughter, Louisa. She married Lord Hope of Hopetoun...such were the benefits of British Chattel Slavery.

The brutal calculations by the sugar barons for the optimal operation of a sugar and rum producing estate such as the Wedderburns' Blue Castle estate in Westmoreland. Jamaica, would be that, 300 black slaves were required to produce 240 tons of sugar and 170 gallons of rum. *The Wedderburn style* of fruity aromatic rum is still produced in Jamaica today and is another legacy of Wedderburn slavery in Jamaica.

Lesser slavers left money that changed their communities and the lives of their descendants. For example, John Newland left slave money to build Bathgate Academy in Scotland in 1833. Robert Waugh, a joiner, made a significant fortune in Jamaica and built Harmony House in Melrose in the Borders region of Scotland in 1807. He became a friend of Sir Walter Scott and gave him financial help. In 1813 the Scottish town of Greenock housed one of the largest sugar businesses in the world. The grand, giant, warehouses that sit, in line, along the shore of Greenock are monuments to a slavery that was meant to last at least a thousand years. The wealth derived from slavery is of no great importance to me. However, what matters is that the countries that were devastated by this outrageous slavery require financial aid to help themselves overcome poverty derived from slavery.

Our heritage is not only related to our slave ancestors it is also linked to the surnames which were derived from slavery. Since they indicate a struggle of which I am proud, why should I give up or deny my lineage. For example, a glance at a Jamaican Telephone Directory shows that about 800 "English" Beckfords and about 2,300 "Scottish" Campbells are listed. This means that there are twice as many Campbells in Jamaica as there are in Edinburgh and surrounding areas. Indeed, there are probably more Campbells per square mile in Jamaica than there are in Scotland. This is not an anomaly. Similar distributions are found for many other English and Scottish names in the West Indies...confirming the long historical links which the West Indies have with Scotland and England. No matter what we feel about our British names...they tell us certain truths about our history and our heritage. Truth can be denied but it cannot be changed. A name does not make us what we are but who would be so ignorant of British -West Indian history to call us "outsiders" and tell us our ancestors played no part in building Britain? We are not recent incomers; we came into Britishness a long time ago when John Hawkins started the British slave trade in 1562 and Bermuda became the first recognised British colony in the West Indies in 1609. We are here to stay.

Towards the end of slavery, British West Indian colonies were packed with slaves. For example, Jamaica's slave population in

1800 was about 300,000. America's slave population in 1800 was about 900,000. Jamaica is about 11,000 Square Kilometres in area: America is about 10,000,000 Square Kilometres in area. At the Emancipation of slavery in 1834, there were about 800,000 slaves in the British West Indies. The growth of this forced transfer of people, from one part of the world to another, against their will, has had a damaging effect on the economy and lives of the people of the West Indies. Notwithstanding, it is worth remembering that by 1800 the West Indies was by far the greatest money earning sector of the British Colonial Empire...contributing four-fifths of the earnings from the Empire. Despite the prejudices of people like Hume, black slaves manned an industry that was larger and more profitable than any operation in Britain at the time.

The soils of these slave lands are now depleted and cannot feed the people. Some people are asking for an apology for slavery. I would prefer grant aid to the West Indies rather than an apology... apologies are often not sincere and if sincere they are expected to remove responsibility. A small number of Churches in Scotland are funding a Jamaican Education Project. This is a good example of what the government should do for that part of the British Empire that gave so much and received so little. The descendants of British slaves that still live in the West Indies have earned the right to be given the help they need to remove the legacies of slavery that limit development.

The most effective help a developing country can have is help that reduces foreign exchange expenditure...this is the kind of help the countries that bled to build Britain during slavery require. That the contributions made by the ancestors of the black descendants of British slavery to Britain are not acknowledged in education and that uninformed civil servants can be consulting on the validity of black identity, contribute to the factors which drive black youths to kill and dishonour each other. This kind of institutional racism wears a mask of mock concern that only fools the gullible. Instead of consulting on identity, why not consult on what is required to ensure that black, minority ethnic as well as deprived white people are provided with the education they need to access their rights in society.

If our children are taught in schools about the fortitude and dignity their black slave ancestors used to survive one of the worst crimes committed against humanity, their self worth would improve. In addition to this, the public need to be informed of how Chattel slavery sustained Britain for nearly 300 years before it was abolished. If this is not done before the end of 2007, the injustices of a long and cruel slavery will continue...and this commemoration will pass into another long period of uneasy silence.

During the commemoration of the ending of the slave trade we have heard long adulations to the abolitionists and the voices of those who are using Chattel slavery to promote "modern slavery". In contrast, the voices of the slaves have been drowned by all these voices of self-interest. The narrative of old Henry's slaves enlightenment (page 52) is an attempt to make us hear the small but significant voices of the slaves that lost their lives on British slave plantations in the West Indies.

Campbells in Jamaica

Campbell Elaine
60 Campbell Elaine
53 Campbell Elaine B
Campbell Elaine E Mrs
46
30 Campbell Elaine E Mrs
L0
Or
58 Campbell Elaine I

L2 Campbell Elaine R

36 Campbell Elaine V

Campbell Elescie L
5
Campbell Elese E
6
0 Campbell Elfreda
Campbell Elfreda A
7
9 Campbell Elfreda K

0 Campbell Elgay
4
0 Campbell Elin G
8 Campbell Elizabeth A

9 Campbell Ellette
5 Campbell-Elliott Lorna D
3
5 Campbell Elma
7
Campbell Elma M
2
Campbell Elorine
2
Campbell Elsada
Campbell Elsie
Campbell Eltis C
Campbell Elveta V
Campbell Emize A
Campbell Ena
Campbell Ena M Mrs

Campbell Enid A
Campbell Enid C
Campbell Enid I
Campbell Enid L
Campbell Enid M
Campbell Enid M
Campbell Enid R
Campbell Enis W
Campbell Enith
Campbell Enthrose

Campbell Era-May

Or
Campbell Eric
Campbell Eric A
Campbell Eric G
Campbell Eric G

RESIDENTIAL

Campbell Ethlyn M

Campbell Ethna H
Campbell Etta
Campbell Etta A

Campbell Eugena B

Campbell Eugenie
Campbell Eugenie

Campbell Eugenie

Campbell Eugenie Mrs

Campbell Eula D
Campbell Eulalee Mrs

Campbell Eulet N

Campbell Eulin
Campbell Euline V

Campbell Eunice
Campbell Eunice I

Campbell Eunice L

Campbell Euva
Campbell Eva
Campbell Evadne
Campbell Evadne E

Campbell Evadne P
Campbell Evadney C

Campbell Evelyn
Campbell Evelyn
Campbell Evelyn

Campbell Evelyn
Campbell Evelyn A

Campbell Evelyn C

Or
Campbell Evelyn D
Campbell Evelyn J Mrs

Campbell Everald
Campbell Everton
Campbell Everton
Campbell Everton D

Campbell Everton E

Campbell Everton L
Campbell Evet M

Campbell Ewart
Campbell Ewen

Campbells in Jamaica

Campbell David J

Campbell David J

Campbell David J
Campbell David N

Campbell David P
Campbell David R

Campbell-Davis Sharon G

Campbell Dawn

Campbell Dawn 1
Campbell Dawn A

Campbell Dawn E

Campbell Dawn E
Campbell Dawnie

Campbell Dean E

Campbell Deanne T

Campbell Deanne T

Campbell Debbie
Campbell Debbieann M

Campbell Deborah A

Campbell Deborah D

Campbell Deita
Campbell Delceta
Campbell Delcita L

Campbell Delleta P

Campbell Delmore

Campbell Delores
Campbell Delores

Campbell Delores

Campbell Delores R
Campbell Delpharine

Campbell Delpharine P

Campbell Delrose

Campbell Delrose E

Campbell Delroy

Campbell Delroy

Campbell Delroy

Campbell Delroy

Campbell Delroy A

Campbell Delroy A

Campbell Devon E

Campbell Devon O
Campbell Devon R

Campbell Dewitt
Campbell Dexter O

Campbell Dezerine
Campbell Diahann R

Campbell Dian A
Campbell Dian A

Campbell Diana E

Campbell Diana I
Campbell Diane S

Campbell Doanld G

Campbell-Dobbs Roxanne J

Or
Campbell Dollis
Campbell Dolrol J

Campbell Donald
Campbell Donald
Campbell Donald
Campbell Donald

Campbell Donald

Campbell Donald C

Campbell Donald K
Campbell Donald L
Campbell Donald M
Campbell Donald O
Campbell Donald S

Campbell Donna 236
Campbell Donna M

Campbell Donna M Mrs

Campbell Donna S
Campbell Donnath

Campbell Donovan

Campbell Donovan

Campbell Donovan
Campbell Donovan

Campbell Donovan F

Campbell Donovan K
Campbell Doran D
Campbell Doreen
Campbell Doreen

Campbell Doreen C

Campbell Doreen M

Letter Home

A LETTER HOME TO BRITAIN
FROM SLAVERY IN JAMAICA

William Adlam was the Supervisor of the Hermitage Slave Estate in St Elizabeth, Jamaica. This is one of the 'routine letters' he wrote home to, a John Weymss of Edinburgh, the Agent of the Moyes estate.

The year 1820 was 13 years after the abolition of the slave trade and 18 years before the abolition of slavery. It is clear that the abolition of the slave trade encouraged the development of the unbelievable practice of breeding people. This is the consequence of applying half-measures in justice... In addition, those who are proud to be 'racist' should read this letter carefully and note the parasitic and barbaric sources of their diseased ideology. Adlam's letter exudes great greed, that is regarded by some as 'enlightened self interest'. However Bonthorn's request for his *Mullato daughter* is evidence that in the midst of the most terrible evil, nature's conscience will emerge to reaffirm our common humanity...

FROM MR ADLAM FEBRUARY 1st - 1820

Dear Sir,

I received your favors of the 29th Oct. and 27th Nov. and fully notice its contents, the supplies for the Hermitage by *Ann Grant* and *St Elizabeth*, also my supplies by *Ann Grant* are arrived and in good order and give satisfaction. The Mill and the Mill house that is required must be deffer'd for some time longer and I hope that the present crop will much better enable us to do it than the last. We shall not have finished crop before the latter end of March, if then, I mean the picking from the field, being rather weak handed we cannot go on as fast as I would wish, by the next packet I can better inform you nearly the number of casks we can make, if we have dry weather for some time to come – to pick in the remainder of the coffee that is in a manner nearly dry, on the trees, for want of strength to pick it when ripe on the trees.

I think we shall make a tolerable good crop, we are now using the old mill and I think will take off this crop without any great expense, or indeed but triffling. I particularly notice your instruction in regard of the shipment of the crop in case it should prove an abundant one – That 10 or 15 tierces should be ship'd to London, or the one half to Glasgow and the other half to Bristol, which I shall attend to.

I think the twenty Casks sold at 96/ per Cwt = of # Coffee sold very low, and hope the coffee in Bristol will meet a better market – the Ball containing 6 pieces oznaburgs for me, the wrapper was much broke and the edge of one of the pieces of oznaburgs rather injured but not much. I think it would be better in future to send it in a Puncheon. As you mention you are particularly anxious to learn the probable extent of the crop this season on Hermitage. I have entertain'd for some time past my opinion that 100 Casks may be made, Mr McLean the Overseer thinks we make 80 Casks and no more, it depends on the weather being favourable in getting the remainder picked, you may partly know from this the extent of the Crop nearly – I have seen Capt. Wilson of the *Ann Grant*, he offered to take from 10 to 15 tons of Ebony at 1 guinea freight per Ton, after getting the Coffee picked in, I intend to set in to cut a few Tons for the *Ann Grant*.

Mr McLean received your letter date 17th Oct. last and my having wrote you an Account of the shirts and shoes disposed off, he thought it would not require any further answer from him to you immediately on the subject – since the receipt of your Letter I have not seen Mr Bonthorn concerning the purchase of his Mullatto Daughter, as we are weak handed on the Hermitage I should prefer his giving a well disposed Man or Woman to the property for her, than purchase her otherwise.

I once mentioned this circumstance to him, but he did not seem inclined to do it. It would be more for the advantage of the property, however I shall be guided by your advice hereon. I am very sorry to inform you we have a few days ago lost an old Invalid Woman named Nancy, she has been doing little or nothing for the property for some time past, and her loss is not much felt in consequence. The women on the Hermitage breed very slow indeed, which I cannot account for, and they are many of them good looking young women. I shall expect to hear from you by next Packet or the *Isabella* – I remain very respectfully

Dear Sir your most obed. Servt.

William Adlam

for articles sold belonging to you, I did not think it so proper to bring it into the Hermitage account with your. The remainder of the things unsold, care shall be taken to endeavour to dispose of them to the best advantage, the Negroes on Hermitage have been and are now sickly, the Doctor left the property last week, and left nine very sick in the Hot house, cheifly with Fevers from the North winds setting in, which is rather unfortunate for us in time of crop, however hope they will soon recover again to go to their work, for every hand is now much wanted, I shall be glad to hear from you again p.ʳ the Ann Grant. Mean time, I remain

Dear Sir

your most obed.ᵗ & humble Serv.ᵗ

William Adlam

From Mr. Adlam Feb: 1ˢᵗ 1820

Dear Sir I received your favor of the 29ᵗʰ Oc.ᵗʳ and 27ᵗʰ Nov and fully notice its Contents, the supplies for Hermitage by Ann Grant and St. Elizabeth, also my supplies by Ann Grant are arrived and in good order and give satisfaction. The Mill and Mill house that is required shantt be defford for some time longer and I hope the present crop will much better enable us to do it than the last, we shall not here finished crop byore the latter end of March, if then, I mean the picking from the field, being rather weak handed we cannot go on as fast as I could wish, by the next packet I can better inform you nearly the number of Casks we can make, if we have dry weather for some time to come — to pick in the remainder of the Coffee that is in a manner nearly dry, on the trees, for want of strength to pick it when ripe on the Trees, I think we shall make a tolerable good crop, we are now using the old Mill and I think will take off this crop without any great expence, or indeed but trifling. I particularly notice your instructions in regard to the shipment of the Crop in case it should prove an abundant one — That 10 or 15 tierces should be ship'd to London, or the one half to Glasgow and the other half to Bristol, which I shall attend to, I think the twenty Casks sold at 96/ per Cwt =

49

of ⟨R⟩ Coffee sold very low, and hope the Coffee in Bristol
will meet a better market — the Ball containing 6 pieces
osnaburgs for me, the wrapper was much broke and the edge
of one of the pieces of osnaburgs rather injured but not much,
I think it would be better in future to send it in a Punch
-eon, As you mention you are particularly anxious to
learn the probable extent of the crop this season on Her
-mitage, I have entertain'd for some time past my opinion
that 100 Casks may be made, Mr McLean the overseer
thinks we may make 80 Casks and no more, it depends
on the weather being favorable in getting the remainder
picked, you may partly know from this the extent of the
Crop nearly, — I have seen Capt. Wilson of the Ann Grant,
he offer'd to take from 10 to 15 Tons of Ebony at 1 Guinea
freight per Ton, after getting the Coffee picked in, I intend
to set in to cut a few Tons for the Ann Grant. Mr McLean
received your Letter dated 17 Octr. last and my having
wrote you an account of the shirts and shoes disposed of,
he thought it would not require any farther answer from
him to you immediately on the subject — since the receipt
of your Letter I have not seen Mr Bonthorn concerning the
Purchase of his Mullatto Daughter, as we are weak handed
on the Hermitage I should prefer his giving a well disposed
Man or Woman to the property for her, than purchase her
otherwise — I once mentioned this circumstance to him,
but he did not seem inclined to do it, It would be more
for the advantage of the property, however I shall be guided
by your advice hereon, I am sorry to inform you we have a
few days ago lost an old Invalid Woman named Nancy,
she has been doing little or nothing for the property for some
time past, and her loss is not much felt in consequence, The
Women on the Hermitage breed very slow indeed, which I
cannot account for, and they are many of them good looking
young women, I shall expect to hear from you by next
Packet or the Isabella — I remain very respectfully
           Dear Sir Your most obed. servt.

                 William Adlam

Slave's Enlightenment

A SLAVE'S ENLIGHTENMENT

*The different voices of the narrator are English, Ebo, Yoruba
and Jamaican patois.*

*In a solemn and dignified voice, old West Indian Henry said
to us: "Be still and listen...*

We were caught, bought, shipped and enslaved
Found hope in God's grace and were saved...
So, why were we not as good as you?

You forced your culture on us in short time
But destroying ours was the greater crime
This dishonouring was long and brutally done
And has made us all what we have become...
So, why were we not as good as you?

During our slavery we had many fears
That your legal codes would kill us
And damage our children for years...
So, why were we not as good as you?
Nyaa, ọ gini bụ na anyi adiro nma ka unu?
Kilode ti awa ko se da to eyin?
Soe, wa mek unu tink unu betta dan we?

You destroyed our families and gave us one name:
Nigger, Quashi
Sambo, Boy
Horatio, Wallace
Sarah, Jane...
Nyaa, ọ gini bụ na anyi adiro nma ka unu?

 You derided our music which was "noise" to your ear
But it gave us a voice that has lasted for years.
You sneered at our colour and laughed at our frame
But we had your children since our blood is the same...
Soe, wa mek unu tink unu betta dan we?

You preached we were 'subhuman but pleasing'
Which Hume and Carlyle confirmed with "reasoning"
But they would not have been clever then
Had they been taught in plantation pens
Soe, wa mek unu tink unu betta dan we?

No writer, preacher, politician of worth
Should have been silent for so long
When kith and kin inflicted such hurt...
Kilode ti awa ko se da to eyin?

Our beaten bodies were sore with pain
Yet you branded and bred us and sold us for gain...
Kilode ti awa ko se da to eyin?

We dug strange fields in New World's dew
And were oft-times sick un-noticed by you
We tried our obeah but it failed
To protect us from the evil that prevailed...
Nyaa, ọ gini bụ na anyi adiro nma ka unu?

What was our price, what was our worth?
To live in a hell you created on earth
You ate or sold the food we grew
And our children died instead of you...
Nyaa, ọ gini bụ na anyi adiro nma ka unu?

Our dead children brought great sorrow
But our steely women were our tomorrow
They were the metal of our arm and eye
That drove us daily to defy...
So, why were we not as good as you?

When we fought and rebelled in our defence
You hanged or slow-burned us for impudence
Often in dark silence we would cry
If this is life, then let us die
And fly from the self interest of the lie...
Kilode ti awa ko se da to eyin?

We ate scraps and lived like rats to survive
But fought and "smiled" to remain alive
We are the "savages" that made you rich
But you buried us in a dirty ditch...
Nyaa, ọ gini bụ na anyi adiro nma ka unu?

You whipped our faces, put filth in our mouths
Which you tied shut, to prevent spitting out.
We endured this "civilised" violence alone
Where your prosperity and prejudices were sown
Only hypocrites and cowards deny their past
Because, good or bad done is meant to last...
Soe, wa mek unu tink unu betta dan we?

Our slavery was a dream rape
From which there was no escape
It was a nightmare come true
A world away and chained by you
The enlightened and the brave
That, "never, never will be slaves"...
So, why were we not as good as you?

Chained, we heard the 12th of April's cannons groan
The hundred year's dice of war was thrown
Again and again we were the prize
In a game of greed you had devised...
Kilode ti awa ko se da to eyin?

Unlike the progenies of animal and grass
Our children will remember the past
But no task on earth is harder
Than to redress the "sins of the Father".
Abolition was not an Act divine,
It was then politic to cover the crime...
Nyaa, ọ gini bụ na anyi adiro nma ka unu?

From masks of mock enlightenment,
            devious people will say:
Others suffered in a similar way
But such denial and cultural play
Will not wash this cruel crime away...
Soe, wa mek unu tink unu betta dan we?

We were not chattel to slave and kill
We have the same humanity:
Love, rage and will...
So, why were we not as good as you?"

For surviving the most profitable evil the world has known
Put up no stone...just repair the damage done, alone.
Our right to be black and live here is not for review...
We paid a bitter price to live like you.

Preface To Britishness

PREFACE

The time of The Enlightenment Abolished gave us the 'reason' of Hume and Rousseau and the racism of New World slavery. Racism is cruel and is the creed of irrational and ignorant people who wrongly believe that skin colour confers superiority. In this regard, many people, whose lives are historically mixed with Britishness, are denied a rightful place in British society because their skin colour is not white. The original concept of Britishness was not about skin colour, it was about a family of different people who shared a political history that emanated from Britain...the rights of these people cannot be changed by racist rhetoric or any other form of nonsense, designed to dishonour black people.

Failure to overcome social racism may indicate that our approaches are incorrect. In order to make meaningful progress, we need to find ways to convert the racists instead of continuing to preach, to small purpose, to the converted. Our racism is not only a cruel legacy of New World slavery: racism is a lie that kills...

The Enlightenment Abolished is neither a history, nor a poem, nor a comment on the pain of the disadvantaged. *The Enlightenment Abolished* is merely a glimpse of one evil event in history...*our slavery*. A large number of people are not aware of the terrible role that their ancestors played in New World slavery. And, although slavery is an important part of their history, it has never been acknowledged or taught. Such neglect tends to support the view that an evil ignored in education is often an event no one wishes to remember. This book is a short narrative of events in the life of a Jamaican immigrant who came to the Mother Country as a boy and believes that New World slavery influences the way we live today and is an essential feature of Britishness. In many ways, our slavery is comparable to other human evils but its cruelty went beyond civilised understanding. This reflection is in the form of a dream. In this dream there are no recommendations for either reparation or revenge…it is a celebration of survival. I have dreamt this dream since I was a carefree child, playing cricket in Race Course in Kingston, Jamaica, on dusty stony ground.

Race Course was a rugged, dangerous and circular waste land in central Kingston where children played and fought and where adults walked during the day and courted and watched cycle racing on Friday nights. Race Course was dusty in the dry season but in the wet season it was covered with a plant that crept along the ground. We called it police macca because, its yellow buttercup-like flower produced a small round fruit covered with thorns which 'arrested' movement when lodged in the soles of our bare feet. One of my weekly jobs in the house was to collect police macca runners which were used to make bush tea for breakfast. Like many other children, I roamed the streets of Kingston, barefooted and without a care. This happened every day except Sundays… on Sundays, I followed my Aunts to Church. Sunday was God's day in Jamaica, that beautiful island of wood and water where slavery was 'legal', long and brutal.

Slavery not only gave us our British way of life, it also gave us our Church that was very large and its walls were deep and solid. The bricks, oak benches, tiles, fittings and a framed poster of Scottish Achievers came from Britain over a period of nearly 170 years. The framed poster was made in a place called Kirkcaldy, in Scotland. My family always sat on the same bench…it was unofficially the Larmond's bench and no one else ever sat there. The pulpit was high up near the organ and the choir, and when the organ broke from old age and overuse, a man came from Britain and made it play again.

Reverend Nichols started my dream. He was sent to us from Britain to be the Minister of our Church. Our Ministers always came from Britain. He was a kindly man. His hair was auburn-brown and my Aunts said that he was as nice looking as King George. His wife had sky blue eyes and wore long floral dresses. When I was at primary school, she gave us buns and powdered milk after the 1951 *Hurricane*. The powdered milk made us sick for a long time. Reverend, as we used to call him, constantly asked us to give our lives to Christ and because we all loved him, we did so nearly every Sunday…but especially on Decision Sunday. He gave me a Sunday school prize once for *Regular Attendance*. However, I had very little input into this attainment. My Aunts' view on Church attendance was simple. If you cannot go to Church, you must be sick and if you are sick then you must take a large dose of castor oil! My Sunday diet of Church attendance was as follows: Morning Service, Sunday School, followed by Night Service. The Church was never silent and its clear voice reassured us…it was our education.

Reverend was the only person we knew who had a car and he took me to the doctor when I was too sick to be cared for by my Aunts. Most of them worked as domestic servants in St Andrews, the then colonial part of town, and could not afford to pay. I was concerned for him because all the Ministers that came to us from Britain died of the fever. When he died we gave him a glorious funeral. I can still hear the metal shoes of the black, black-plumed horses slipping on the wet, worn tramlines, as his funeral carriage turned from Princess Street into North Street. He did not want to be taken back to Britain so we buried him in the Churchyard. Every Sunday, after Sunday school, I used to sit on the cool marble of his tombstone and watch people pass and trams trundle by. In season, the large red flowers of the Royal Poinciana would shed their golden pollen on his grave. We called this grand tree the cassha tree because of the noise its long, dry fruit pod made when shaken in fun or in playful fights.

I often remember the Reverend at Christmas Service preaching in the breaking light of the day. My Aunts would wake me at 5 a.m. and we dressed ourselves, in our *Sunday-best*, for Church in the fluttering light of the oil lamp and walked, in silence, the long distance to Church. At East Street we passed the ghostly old colonial house, with its large twin stairs and high garden walls. The service was held earlier than usual so that the children could go downtown to Christmas Market at Queen Victoria's Park. There were other services that I remember: There was the solemnity and calmness of our Three Hours Service on Good Friday with my Aunts propping me up as I fell asleep. There were the flickering magical candles of Candle Light Service; the aromatic smells of the fresh fruits and bread of Harvest Service and the noisy Friday Morning Services when all the school children gathered in the Church for a bit of pushing and shoving but mostly for praying and singing. Reverend Nichols will always be at the centre of these kind and gentle memories.

The activities of Mr Chen's corner shop reflected some of the special events of the Church. He sold raisin-filled buns and Cheddar cheese at Easter, specially moulded breads at Harvest and large rum-raisin cakes at Christmas. Among other things, he sold Cadbury's milk chocolate, Kellogg's corn flakes, potato crisps, Libby's tropical fruit salad, Camp coffee, Fry's cocoa, Lipton's tea, hot peppery patties (spicy descendents of the Scottish bridie) and Tate and Lyle's white granulated sugar, which were 'exported' from Britain. I used to add this list of expensive 'ethnic' food products to my requests from God in my daily prayers, but they never materialised while I was in Jamaica! However, sometimes my Aunts would weaken and buy treats such as wet-salted pig's tail and dry-salted codfish (saltfish), which also came from Britain.

The salted pig's tail was made into a stew which we ate with yams or boiled rice. The salt fish was cooked with akee (ackee) and eaten with boiled or roasted breadfruit. Both these plants were brought to the island, in 1778 and 1793 by Admiral Rodney and by Captain Bligh respectively to feed black people that were described by our teachers as…'the slaves'. Reverend told us that Jamaica was discovered by Columbus in 1494 but had been part of the British Empire since 1655, long before the creation of the Union of Great Britain, and that Britain was the *Mother Country* embodying and respecting diversity in a family of different cultures. Jamaica won its independence in 1962 but many important ties remain, with regard to our religion, language, education, laws and black and white ancestry.

Throughout its long history, Jamaica has been poor, proud, and defiant against injustice (as at the Morant Bay Rebellion in 1865). The two Jamaican heroes of this rebellion were Paul Bogle and George Gordon. Their Scottish surnames relate to the slave heritage of these great men whose Britishness made them realise that rights denied required personal sacrifice to be achieved. Therefore, as free men, they fought for the right to live with dignity, just as the Tolpuddle Martyrs had done in England a few years before in 1834, one year after slavery was abolished. The Tolpuddle Martyrs were transported…but Jamaican Martyrs, Bogle and Gordon (1865) and Samuel Sharpe (1832) were hanged. The terrible torture that Jamaicans suffered during and after slavery never grew into disloyalty. They fought for the Empire when called and, as a boy, I remember the warm welcome we gave Winston Churchill. The welcome was as warm as a tropical summer's day and equal to the welcome we gave to Haile Selassie. Churchill sat on the back seat of a big black car with the Governor, Sir Hugh Foot, the brother of Michael Foot, a past leader of the Labour party. Churchill smoked a large Jamaican cigar and waved two fingers in the sign of a 'V'. I did not know what this meant but we waved our Union Jacks for him as we did for the Queen when she was crowned in 1952.

Jamaica is one of the best known islands in the world and has been given a degree of attention that compares only to the unfair size of the poverty that it now endures. To many, the perception is that Jamaica is that musical place, associated with drugs and violence. This is a small and lopsided view of a country that has contributed more wealth to the world than it will ever receive, while enduring a most pernicious slavery for hundreds of years. A deprivation that it now bears alone. Like the majority of any society, most Jamaicans are against crime and, by world standards, the comparatively small but unacceptable transport of drugs into Britain from Jamaica has damaged a long historical relationship, causing a British visa system to be imposed on the island in 2003.

The majority that obey the law should not be made to suffer because of the illegal folly of the few. That we who slaved for Britain without pay should now have to fill in visa forms and take citizen tests, is to us 'the worst of sins'.

Reverend Nichols believed that reading was better than writing and arithmetic because reading enabled us to read the Bible. He also believed in what he called British order and contentment, so he made us form long queues round the Church and the School, and with vigorous conducting, taught us to sing songs in rounds, such as: 'Rule Britannia' (that strangely boastful song, written by the Scot, James Thomson during slavery), 'Row Boys Row', 'O, my love's like a red, red rose', written by the great Scottish poet, Robert Burns, who applied to be a slave master in Jamaica), 'Who is Sylvia', 'Loch Lomond', 'Where the bee sucks', 'I'll Be A Sunbeam For Jesus', 'Amazing Grace' (that popular hymn written by John Newton an ex-slaver), and many others, including, 'Eternal Father, Strong To Save'. The latter song was usually sung for people who were emigrating to 'better themselves' in America or Britain. They sang it for my Mother and her cousin, in 1948, when I was eight and for me on the Sunday before I left for London to find a job to help my Mother. I was fourteen years old. My father went to America to pick oranges in 'farm working' when I was six years old but we never heard from him and according to my Aunts, "God provides for you so *He* is your Father." However, when my father died in New York thirty seven years later, my Aunts and my Mother were content that I went to Harlem to bury him.

As a child in Jamaica, 'bettering oneself' also meant attending a private secondary school and taking examinations such as, Cambridge School Certificate or Scottish Matriculation and Highers. These were controlled by Examination Boards in England and in Scotland, respectively. This route to 'betterment' required money that was beyond the means and possibilities of most of us. Therefore, we took our shiny blue-black British Passports and, with British 'on your bike' initiative, boarded expensive British Cunard line boats and B.O.A.C. planes and travelled to find work in the Eldorado of our dreams…*the Mother Country*.

My Mother was my Mother but my Aunts mothered me, especially my cousin Liz's mother. Her name was Aunt Agatha but I called her Mama Gatha. She often intervened when punishment sessions became extensive and smiled as she helped me to read the Bible. My mother sailed from Jamaica on the *Mauritania* on a clear, but windy day. The brown baby seagulls whistled for food and the humming birds dallied in the breeze. Important losses that we cannot change must be coped with and endured.

The snow sparkled like jewels in the night-light when she arrived in London. No-one would rent her a room, so the Salvation Army took her in. She worked hard in menial jobs, lived on very little, and never took a holiday. My Grandaunt and my Aunts looked after all the children in the family. The small amount of money my Mother sent to them from Britain helped to feed my brother and me. Her postal orders always came in blue Air-letters which gave up their contents of money only after being torn to bits! My Aunts were my Mother's eight sisters – she was the youngest. My Mother also had an elder brother, uncle Ferdy. I met him for the first time when he returned from Panama. He was a labourer on the Panama Canal. He had many gold teeth and dressed neatly. His clothes smelt of moth balls. There was a 'bosi' air about him... he knew the ways of the world and we did not...

My Grandaunt would not let him live in the house so he lived down the street…she did not want a man in her house! My uncle's main aim was 'to discipline me'…this meant a beating for any misdemeanour. Somehow, I managed to keep out of his reach but we eventually became friends when one-day he asked me if I could see Gabriel in the ackee tree. "Can you see his armour of gold?" he implored. Looking carefully into the dancing leaves of the tree, I said, "Yes, uncle." He patted me on the head and said, "If you can see Gabriel, you must be a good boy..." My Aunts, my Mother and uncle were born in New Green (named so by slave masters from Greenock, Scotland). They left school at 11 years of age. The small piece of land where they were born is called Marshalls Pen. It was acquired by their ancestors from their 'owners', the Lamonds of Argyll, Scotland, at the end of slavery.

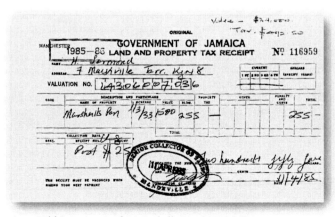

Aunt Hilda's tax receipt for Marshalls Pen (1985-86)

The first time I saw Marshalls Pen, the earth was broken, red and almost dead. It had been sucked dry to an inch of its long life by too many crops of colonial-grown coffee and sugar. My Mother's surname was Larmond. Her great grandfather, at the end of slavery, took his owner's surname and called himself Larmond instead of Lamond. His slave name was Henry, and when he was freed he called himself Henry Larmond. He and his male descendants described their professions as planters...a profession they regarded as important because slave masters called themselves planters. As in Scottish tradition, his Christian name, Henry, has been passed down to eldest sons, so my Mother gave me Henry as one of my names. Our names are an important part of the history of Britishness and provide a permanent link between us and the contributions our ancestors made to the British Empire. What's in a name?...a history which confers rights that cannot be changed. Henry is one of the names of my grandson. He was born in Edinburgh.

When my Mother's parents died, my Grandaunt took her sister's children (my Mother and my Aunts) to Kingston to live with her at 37 John Street in Allman Town, because the land was depleted. It could no longer support them. Allman Town is known for its poverty, but it has always been of great pride to me because Marcus Garvey (1887 - 1940), the great promoter of black potential, was a local government representative for Allman Town.

My Grandaunt used to say that our main purpose in life is to love God and to make sure that no-one suffers or dies from hunger or human cruelty. Like my Mother and my Aunts, my Grandaunt loved a good funeral. She loved the equality of death and the exclusivity of heaven. "Only the chosen-good will be admitted," she would sigh with closed eyes. My Aunts and Mother were devout Christians even though they did not disregard the powers of obeah. They saw death as the rest they worked for all their lives. My Mother came alive at family weddings and funerals. Although she was ill we travelled together to Jamaica to bury her brother. She took me to examine the coffin and prodded the lining and told the undertaker that it was not plush enough and had to be replaced. She prepared her brother for burial using a mixture of customs passed on from previous generations. I knew I would be the last generation to do this...emigration to Britain at fourteen years of age damaged the link between custom and practice in our culture.

My Aunts fed me, clothed and cared for me with a string of Victorian commands: children are to be seen and not heard...do what you are told to do...small boys don't talk back...only men wear under-pants and you are a boy...eat what you are given...don't eat from strangers, they can obeah you...don't tear your clothes... learn your three Rs, but too much learning will damage your eyes and your brain...we will feed you, teachers will teach you and the Reverend will save your soul, so saith the Lord...manners maketh the man...don't talk when you eat...honour thy Mother...sweep the yard...stain and shine the floor...haste makes waste...feed the dogs...The Lord loves obedient children...ingratitude is the worst of sins...spare the rod and spoil the child...you will go to Stoney Hill if you don't behave...keep your head up... don't bear false witness...go to bed, Big Ben and the BBC's Mr Stamp say it is 9 of the clock...say your prayers... you will get a beating if you keep saying cha (pshaw) and suck your teeth like the slaves used to do... and remember, God is not sleeping.

My Grandaunt was called *Auntie* and everyone loved and respected her. She was tall, mysterious, wore a brimmed hat on top of her grey, curly hair and she read her bible every day. Her skin was pale as moonlight and her eyes were blue-green like the sea, but my Grandaunt's sister's skin and eyes were velvet black. We all differed in colour, shape and form but the significance of such differences had no meaning until we arrived in London where the 'Keep Britain White' graffiti confirmed general antipathy to our colour and as some newspapers fanned the flames of prejudice, the 'Black Shirts' and others attacked us. Two politicians were particularly unpleasant. Powell despised us because we, a tiny powerless minority, would somehow cause 'rivers of blood'. Nabarro, a comparatively recent Citizen of the Empire, cynically resurrected the slave-derived propaganda of 'the dangers of black sexuality'. With unbridled hate he stated that white girls would destroy their families' well-being by taking home big black men to tea.

Prejudice comes in many guises: some expected, others as surprising as the racism of the late Philip Larkin, who was recorded singing with gusto and low-life malice, "Throw the Niggers out." We expect this from ignorant people but surely not from 'a poet of the people' who wrote about the rights of humanity. Racists are not born, they are made in the society which they damage. In this regard, for a white ex-football manager to call a black footballer a "lazy Nigger" and then try to excuse his dishonouring of black people by stating that he helped black footballers in the past, shows that he does not understand that it is wrong to belittle people, no matter what one has done for them.

Nigger: Where does the word come from? It came from the harrows of New World slavery. As such, white people, whether prattler or poet, should be ashamed to speak it; but black people should be proud to hear it. The word Nigger is the evidence of a great brutality that came from white slavers like Thomas Thistlewood, a friend of fellow slaver, James Wedderburn. Thistlewood was a Jamaica-based English slave master during a period of The European (Scottish) Enlightenment (1750-1786). His numerous sexual partners were black female slaves. They bore him children in between torture. He documented, in detail, his criteria for purchasing slaves: "Negroes that have big bellies, ill shaped legs, and great feet are commonly dull and sluggish and not often good; whereas those who have good calf to their leg and a small moderate size foot, are commonly nimble, active Negroes...Have also observed that many new Negroes, who are bought fat and sleek from the ship, soon fall away much in a plantation, whereas those which are in a moderate condition hold their flesh better and are commonly hardier. Those whose lips are pale, or whites of their eyes yellowish, are seldom healthy". The word Nigger came out of this evil...an evil that changed the name, Negro to Nigger. Those who use the word Nigger as a weapon of abuse are pathetic little people of low self-esteem and great ignorance.

Another prominent racist during this modern period of racial torture was Sir Keith Joseph. At an interview for my first research position in 1964, he suggested that I should go back to Trinidad. I said I was from London, not Trinidad. With a blatant disregard of what I had said, he suggested that I should go there and grow bananas. Not one member of the interview panel intervened. He then asked with measured malice, "How can bananas produce new bananas when they have no seeds?" I replied slowly, "They have suckers." The mockery continued. Knowing that I had never been on a farm he asked, "What is the difference between a wheat field and a barley field?" I did not know that then! The inevitable, "I regret to inform you letter" followed. I took it with a sigh and moved on with a smile: my *system consciousness* was in the process of development.

Gradually, it became clear to me that social justice cannot be achieved without an understanding of how the system works. Also, it was evident that the most dangerous people in society are those who are in a position to make a difference but prevent others from achieving.

At that time, it was distressing to realise that ignorance of the concepts of Britishness caused apparently fair-minded people to vote in a racist manner. Denial of the basic concepts of Britishness, which embodies differences in race and culture and reflects historical links rather than skin colour, will destroy the meaning of Britishness. Such dangerous disregard for democracy and fairness has stifled the development of peace and trust in the community. At that time we, who were proud of our British heritage, were paid less and charged more to live and the racists, with their contrary logic, labelled us: job-takers, slum-makers, house owners, aggressive ganja scroungers with loud music, prone to insanity, susceptible to arrest, religious and educationally sub-normal. Black parents' enthusiasm for education was seriously damaged by white teachers, who dismissed their hopes for their children as 'unrealistic expectations'.

Attempts to meet the educational needs of black children were viewed in some quarters as 'unfair benefits to foreigners', in social situations where low expectations were the norm. Sadly, these unjust and jealous reactions are still at the centre of present day racist response to the legitimate rights of ethnic people. Irrespective of colour, class or creed, children tend to perform below their educational potential if negative attitudes pervade their schools and where they live.

My expectations were modest on the day I arrived at the Liverpool Docks on the Cunard line ship, *Ascania*, in 1955. I was fourteen years old and my passport said that I was a citizen of the British Empire. My trip started at the Palisadoes airport in Jamaica. I was too young to leave Jamaica alone by ship but I was permitted to fly to New York and board the *Ascania* from there. I had not been to the airport before and had only ever seen a plane flying overhead. On the night of my departure my Grandaunt called me to her rocking chair. The dogs were asleep and the house was quiet. She put down her newspaper and said a prayer and anointed my head with oil. She then told me to remove my shirt. She picked up her newspaper, *The Daily Gleaner,* and wrapped it round my chest and tied it in place with sisal string. I then replaced my shirt, took up my small suitcase and jumped on the back of Mr. Green's truck. My Aunts sat on the veranda and said nothing. I cannot remember if they waved but I knew they would miss me and that I would miss them. Our response to this parting was not displayed in hugs and kisses, we did not show our feelings in public or private.

At the Palisadoes airport I jumped down from the back of the truck and eventually I was on the plane. It was very large and had four propeller-driven engines. Many of the people spoke a language I did not understand. I had not heard a foreign language before. The newspaper under my shirt and the heat of the plane caused me to sweat and by the time we arrived in Florida I was soaking wet. They told us to get off the plane. I had not seen so many lights before. They lined us up in the half-light and began asking questions: Are you a communist? Have you ever been to a communist gathering? Do you know any communists? The man in front of me said no, so I said no. We re-boarded the plane. In New York it was very cold. Steam came out of the streets. There were about twenty four Jamaicans on the plane. They confined us to a cage-like enclosure.

One of my Mother's sisters who lived in New York threw me her husband's overcoat over the fence. I was shaking and the wet newspaper round my chest began to get very cold. I put on the overcoat and could hardly walk because it was too long. They herded us, stumbling, onto a bus and drove us towards the ship. I had never seen so many cars before. When we arrived at the Hudson River Docks, a guard with a machine gun, whose job it was to prevent us from escaping into America, opened the back door of the bus and told us to get out and walk through Immigration. I eventually found my bed on the boat. There were six of us to a room on the bottom deck of the ship. I went to the toilet and removed the wet newspaper from my chest; my Grandaunt would certainly not know what I had done!

The *Ascania* sailed down the Hudson river past the Statue of Liberty and out to sea. The sea was rough. We were sick many times and could not eat the food, which was mainly pasta. One Jamaican man continually asked me, "What is this kind of food?" I said that I did not know. We sailed and docked at our first port...some of us thought we had arrived in Liverpool but later learned that this port was Nova Scotia. I got off the ship and walked on snow for the first time. The snow was so deep that they had to cut it away to show the windows and doors of the shops. The whole place looked like a giant Christmas card. I made and threw a snowball as I had seen people do in a film. I returned to the ship and we sailed for Liverpool. The sea boiled with anger and the ship tilted from side to side and some of us on the lowest deck of the ship nearly died from vomiting.

As we sailed towards Liverpool, I began to explore the upper decks of the ship. Only white people occupied the upper decks. When they were not gambling they were eating or dancing. One day a lady called me into a large room, she was playing cards with other ladies. Another lady put me on her knee and asked me if I was hungry. I said yes. She wrapped up a tray full of sandwiches and a tray full of pieces of fruit cake and gave them to me. I took these down to my Jamaican friends and we ate the cake and sandwiches quickly. I made my trip to the upper deck almost daily. Each time I brought back a bounty of cake and sandwiches. About ten days after leaving New York the ship reached Cork. It did not dock, it anchored out at sea. Many Irish people sailed out in small boats to meet the ship and they tried to sell us beads and trinkets! It became dark and we sailed for Liverpool with great apprehension and arrived there on the 10th March 1955...coincidentally, the 10th March is the same day, that I was given the honour, fifty years later, to return to Kingston, Jamaica, to address the Jamaica Chamber of Commerce.

After we left the docks at Liverpool, I went through Immigration with my small twenty six shillings suitcase. My grey-blue overcoat dragged on the ground as I walked. At Immigration I was asked if I had any guns or drugs. I said no. As we boarded the train I could still see the steep wall of the ship. I found a seat on the ship-train and stared out of the window as it sliced its way quickly through the flowing countryside. Soon we arrived at a large station in London. It was crowded and noisy and I stood in the half-light and looked around until a lady came and grabbed my arm with the words, "Godfrey, come with me, I am your Mother..." I did not recognise her because she left Jamaica when I was eight years old and now I was fourteen years and eleven months old.

We boarded a red bus and got off at Pentonville Prison, Caledonian Road in North London. The falling snow soaked into my flimsy shoes before we reached the front door where my Mother lived. It was very dark and my Mother could not find the hole in the door to insert the key. The landlord said hello and my Mother took me up three flights of stairs to her attic room. She turned on the light and lit the paraffin heater. Her bed was against one wall and my bed was against the opposite wall. She went out to the stair landing where the cooker was, shooed a rat that was curled up asleep on the cooker and then cooked corn beef and rice, which I ate before I brushed my teeth and went to sleep. My Mother read her Bible, said her prayers and then went to bed. I had not said my prayers from the day I left Jamaica. I said goodnight but did not know what to call her...this is just one small way in which the need to make a living disrupts the lives of poor people.

The next morning, the clock's alarm went at 6.00 a.m. My Mother switched on the light and shouted at me to get up. She turned on the radio to confirm the time and prepared herself for work. After washing, I got dressed, ate two slices of bread, drank a mug of real (green) tea and followed my Mother down the stairs in silence. Most of the other tenants in the house had already gone to work. My Mother opened the front door…a white man barred our way. He was dressed in a pinstripe suit and carried a brown briefcase. It was about 6.45 a.m. "Is the name of this boy, Godfrey Palmer ?" asked the man. "Yes," replied my Mother. "Where are you going ?" asked the man. "To work," said my Mother. "You can go to work, but the boy cannot," he warned. "Why not?" asked my Mother. "Because he is not fifteen years of age, and in this country all children have to go to school until they are at least fifteen…is that clear?"

My Mother realised that her plans to take me to work had failed and she began to beg the man to be lenient. She implored, "I, Sir, have been in this country since 1948. I have worked nights sorting mailbags for less than three pounds ten shillings a week. Now I only have two pounds ten shillings a week to live on and, I have this boy in London to feed and another younger boy in Jamaica to feed and I do not have a man to help me. My son's fare to London cost me £86 and this took me from 1948 to 1955 to save…my son has to work to help me." "He can get a paper round…or a Saturday job, but he must go to school…I don't make the rules," he concluded, firmly.

He gave my Mother a piece of paper on which the names of various schools were written. That same day my Mother took me to Barnsbury Comprehensive School and they gave me a test and the results indicated that I was 'educationally sub-normal'. I was sent to Shelburne Road Secondary Modern and they accepted me.

Mr. Bullen was the Headmaster of Shelburne Road School. He took me on the grounds that I would stay longer than the month required to take me to my fifteenth birthday in April, because he did not want me to 'ruin the Register'! It was agreed that I stayed until June 1955. At Shelburne, some parents abused some teachers and some teachers smirked at the poor abilities of the pupils and some pupils fought each other at break-time. It was the time of the Teddy boy gangs and I used my experience of the streets in Jamaica to avoid trouble. There was an ease about education at Shelburne. In one 'maths' lesson we had to cut out pictures of furniture, give them prices then add up the total cost. The music teacher was wolf-whistled when she came into the room and the old history teacher started many lessons by glaring at the teddy boys. He would then repeat, "At the war front, it was the bullies that were afraid to fight." At that time 'racism' was directed mainly at the Jews. The main derogatory comment in the playground was, 'You dirty Jewboy'. However, in a short while this seemed to change to 'Coon' and 'You bloody Nigger'.

At Shelburne I excelled at scripture and cricket but it was cricket that played the most significant part in changing my life. Two months after joining Shelburne I was playing cricket in the playground. The games-master stopped me and said that I should meet him after school on Wednesday. On Wednesday he gave me a pair of white gym shoes and he took me, by train, to a place called Gants Hill. It was a large park and there were many boys there accompanied by their parents carrying large cricket bags. I did not understand the purpose of this event but I was asked to bowl and bat which I did. The games-master and I left and returned home. Two weeks later, I was called by the games-master, who told me calmly, "You have been selected to play for London…you are now a member of the London Schoolboys Cricket Team…"

The games master gave me a white shirt and white flannels he had collected, and another teacher gave me a pair of white canvas boots. The fixtures of the team included: Eton, Harrow, Winchester and Middlesex Colts. The significance of these names escaped me at the time. I merely turned up, went on long coach rides, played cricket and returned home to Bride Street which was near Pentonville Prison. The vastness of the playing fields at Eton was exciting and I have not forgotten the boy who looked after me at Harrow. I was allocated to him when I got off the coach. He said, "Hello," and asked if I would like to see his dorm…I said, "Yes," but did not quite know what he meant. As we walked across the grass I thought that this must be a school for poor boys because he had a straw hat…to me this view was confirmed fully when he showed me where he slept ! There were many iron bunk beds in the room, the floor was wooden and not even covered with linoleum. It was fairly cold…and not a paraffin heater in sight. He asked me, "And what does your daddy do ?" I replied cheerfully, "Well he is in New York and I have been told he runs numbers…a sort of a gambling racket." "Ah," he said, in great astonishment, "My Daddy does the same…he's in the City." We had a good game at Harrow and we won.

Like the Church, the game of cricket filled me with awe and worry. I did not have a scrapbook of The Apostles but I had a large scrapbook of great cricketers and tried to copy the different styles in which they played the game. I had only ever watched two days of test match cricket during my childhood in Jamaica. Both times I was helped to climb over the high wall of the Sabina Park cricket ground. I was one of a large group of boys who were trying to get over the wall because we had no money.

The only price I paid to watch these matches was a twisted ankle because the jump down, into the grounds, was about ten feet. I saw the West Indies play England. Of the cricketers I saw in Jamaica, I will never forget the grace of Frank Worrell and Len Hutton; the craft of Denis Compton; the power of Everton Weeks and the controlled aggression of Clyde Walcott. Nor will I forget the safe hands of Godfrey Evans, the smooth running and delivery of Hines Johnson; the erratic speed of Freddie Trueman; the accuracy of Alec Bedster and Lance Gibbs, and the magical spin bowling of Sonny Ramadhin. I also had the special privilege to see the last test match of the great George Headly. He had passed his best and made only one run.

Cricket can be elating but there is the dark side of the game. All those who have played cricket are aware of its terrors…the nervous knee-shaking walk to the wicket, the intimidation of the fielders, the being out for nought, the slow long walk back to the silence of team members that one has let down, the dropped catch and the thrashing received without taking a wicket. Then there was the minister of the Church that acted as umpire. He sent me off the field for 'technical dissent'. When I complained that I was never sent off in Jamaica for dissent…he smiled and said, "You do here!" All these hazards of the game conspired to convince me that hereafter I should only play this very British game, that changed my life for the better, for pleasure.

In July or August 1955, the Islington Gazette published an article which said that Shelburne had produced a valuable schoolboy cricketer that was playing for London. Mr. King, the headmaster of the local grammar school must have seen the article and asked Mr. Bullen, the headmaster of Shelburne, to transfer me to Highbury County School. My Mother was again disappointed that the grocery boy's job she had arranged for me would fall through but accepted the £5 per term which she received to help pay for my school uniform which I was required to wear at Highbury.

Before I went to Highbury, I got a temporary job, to supplement my paper round money, at Fasbender and Evans, a leather handbag firm, in the East End of London. I lined sections of handbags with satin. Each day the foreman would pick five of us from the work floor and send us to the toilet for 'rest periods'. When I asked him why we had to do this, he replied firmly, "To save jobs, Sunshine…to save jobs." I left the job to go to Highbury School at the beginning to the Autumn term of 1955.

When I entered Highbury, I was the only black pupil. When I left in 1958 there were two black pupils, a boy called Michael Phillips and me. He was from Guyana and told us that he knew Latin. The only other pupils from the Empire at the school were Theofanides and Papapetrou - they were Greek-Cypriots. Osman was a Turkish-Cypriot and Cardozo was from Burma. Phillips did not play cricket or football. Theo and Papa played football. We were all of the British Empire and we got on well but the Cypriots argued bitterly over Cyprus.

Mr King, the headmaster, knew how we were affected by local hardships and the politics of the British Empire. This may have influenced him in permitting us to put on a dance in the school. We made a large profit and bought the school a small silver cup out of part of the profit! We called it the Commonwealth Cup. I have been told that Highbury now has mainly ethnic pupils and a cup called the Commonwealth Cup is given for team work.

Mr. King was a kindly man and devoted himself to the education of deprived children. He allowed me to run two paper rounds from which I earned £1 per week. I gave my Mother ten shillings, sent three shillings to my Grandaunt in Jamaica and kept seven shillings for my lunch and spending money. Instead of throwing out 'slow learners and troublemakers', he assembled them in a special class called The Removes. I was in The Removes and so were most of my friends, except a boy called Bob Green who has remained a very close friend. Bob introduced me to beer and I introduced him to the music of Shirley and Lee and other Blues singers. Nearly all the members of the school's cricket and football teams came from The Removes. Our maths teacher, Mr Lewis, disliked us and often humiliated us by asking us to solve problems we could not solve. One day he stopped me in the playground and said, "Where are you from, boy?" "Jamaica, sir." " Must be hot there in Africa this time of year, what, what!" "Yes, sir…" Unlike Mr Lewis, Corporal (Mr) Gage, the games master, was more charitable. He called all of us 'dirty scumbags' because our gym shoes were dirty! When I told him that my Mother did not want me to swim because of an ear ache, he retorted, "Do I tell your Mother how to bake a cake!" I never did learn to swim.

My academic performance at Highbury was patchy. I was not familiar with the concepts of science subjects such as chemistry, physics and mathematics and struggled to cope but I did reasonably well at scripture, history, geography and biology. Achievement in science required experience which I did not have but I liked English Literature mainly because one of our teachers, Mr. Ward, made us muddle through Steinbeck, Hemingway and Faulkner in the class, whether we liked it or not. It took me some time to understand what he was trying to do but having had to read the Bible all my life, the stories of these writers probably made more sense to me than they did to some of the other boys. However, the main purpose of my 'transfer' to Highbury was to play cricket and football and this I did frequently and relatively well!

My school days at Highbury ended in 1958. I had passed a few 'O' level and two 'A' level examinations. Of the many events that happened at Highbury, I will remember that my friend Bob and I were among London children sent to the country for a few days to broaden their outlook of Britain. Roaming around the streets of a town called Oswestry, Bob and I went into a pet shop and ordered two birds…he wanted an archaeopteryx and I wanted a pterodactyl. The owner smiled at us quizzically and after searching through a book said, "We have had a run on these…very popular these foreign birds…but we can get them in if you wish." "No sir," we said, "we are leaving the country soon." The biology teacher then enquired at the counter what we were up to. He was not amused and threatened to cane us to within an inch of our lives. I left school before my luck ran out! Bob went to work for the Bank of West Africa somewhere in London but did not stay long. He is now Chairman of his own company in the United States. I did not have a job so I went to the Islington Public Library every day, except Sundays, to read the papers and keep warm.

I have been told many times, "You must have worked hard to achieve what you have achieved." Hard work, without support from others is not enough to make significant gains in life, especially in education. I have had the help of many 'Good Samaritans' in my life. One was Professor Garth Chapman. He gave me my first job in 1958. I was a junior technical assistant at Queen Elizabeth College. I did odd jobs in the department. He encouraged me to discuss the difficulties, which were causing my poor attendance at work. The Prof. understood how people like myself had to live so he refused to confirm my dismissal. When he realised that, at eighteen, I was defending my Mother in court from being evicted from our home, he encouraged me to study the function of the court and the meaning of the rent act. We won the case. The landlord had to stop the continual noise, re-connect our water supply and desist from starting fights. Indeed, the bucket I used to collect our daily drinking and washing water from across the road now grows plants. Our rent was half my Mother's wage which was five pounds per week. She worked as a dress finisher for Mr. Kafka in the East End of London, and received a box of Woolworths' chocolate at Christmas, if she did not miss a day's work during the year.

After we won the court case, the Prof. said that I should complete my university entrance examinations and try to enter university by 1961. I did not want to go to university to fail. I did not know how I would relate with people who did not have my background. Passing the racists at Notting Hill Gate each day on my way to and from work, was less of a problem. During this period, I did not know any West Indian students. They wore scarves and told white people that they were different from us immigrants. But after the riots in Notting Hill Gate (1958) they became immigrants because white racists treated us all the same...black was black! When I failed to secure a place in any university in Britain Professor Chapman argued my case and consequently I got a place at Leicester University in 1961. Seeds will not find furrows and grow in impossible soil...likewise, my efforts alone were not enough even though I had met the entrance requirements of various universities and held a County Major Grant Award from the London County Council. Before I left my job for Leicester, the Prof., with the anger of the just, advised me thus, "In future, never send a photograph with any application form. This contrivance should not be necessary in a civilised society but it may induce prejudiced people to read at least part of your application form before they reject you!" Despite the concept that the rights of the minority must not conflict with the expectations of the majority, a true democracy exists to defend the rights of both the majority and the minority. Professor Chapman was a great egalitarian. Sadly he died in 2003.

I returned to London after gaining my first degree at Leicester University in Botany in 1964. I did not know what my degree qualified me to do. One of my friends from the streets reasoned that Botany was like gardening and suggested that I asked at Finsbury Park what kind of work was available. I decided to work with my Uncle Se, the husband of Aunt Kate. Uncle Se had a house in Marlborough Road and most of the family lived in the house…my Mother and I did not. He loved Scotch whisky and his work. However, he was not pleased that in Jamaica he was called a carpenter but in London he was called a joiner! We did many different kinds of work: cleaning sewers, plastering, wood and cement work and decorating. I helped but had no expertise at all. It is difficult to recount all the jobs we completed but I remember filling gaping holes in dusty wattle walls with newspapers and plastering them into the wall. I became more and more nervous regarding the quality of our work and finally 'resigned' when a night club owner threatened to kill us because his heavy Hessian (Japanese) wall paper fell off the wall after two days… Uncle Se's view was that we were lucky, the owner would have killed us had he paid us! After Uncle Se's house was damaged mysteriously by bottles, and the police failed to respond to our call, I decided that my career as a decorator was over and my search for a real job began at the Seven Sisters Road Labour Exchange in London.

At the partition grid of the Labour Exchange, I was questioned by a man. He exuded that kind of indifference that numbs the mind. He looked at me and smirked, "Any skills, any qualifications?"

I said that I had a degree. He rocked on his chair and laughed. Turning to his colleague he sniggered, "Hi here, Paddy, this one reckons he has a temperature!" He gave me a slip of paper…one job was for a park attendant in Finsbury Park, the other job was for a potato peeler at Beales restaurant in Holloway Road, London.

At Beales, the old lady who peeled the potatoes told me that this job would get me far. She had done it for thirty years and because I looked a bright boy there were no good reasons why I could not do it for a similar period. I enjoyed my job at Beales. Among the many things I learnt, I remember two vividly: one of the cooks admonished me because I was about to throw away a bowl of fruit salad that had been returned by a customer. He took the bowl containing the limp-looking fruit salad and added a bright red cherry to the centre of the fruit salad in the bowl and sent it back down to the restaurant…the same customer ate the fruit salad and did not complain. The cook then smiled at me and said, "Most people judge on appearance, mate… they usually see what they want to see, not what is there…get my drift!" The other lesson I learnt was that when the same cook asked for 'new potatoes' he meant that I should hunt through the damp mound of 'old potatoes' to find 'small old potatoes'! I applied for many jobs during my time at Beales and was finally accepted at the Heriot-Watt College (now a University) and Edinburgh University in 1964 by Professor Anna MacLeod, to study for a joint PhD in grain science and technology, at the beginning of 1965.

I met many West Indian students in Edinburgh. They were high achievers who came directly to universities in Britain and usually returned to the West Indies after completing their studies. The late Bernie Grant, who became a Member of Parliament for the Labour Party, did not return to Guyana. He went from Edinburgh to London and established himself as a prominent politician in the area of race relations. The last time Bernie came to Edinburgh was to discuss the entry of his son into university. Before he left for London we had a drink in a pub in Duddingston. Sadly, the higher fees paid by overseas students have almost stopped this tradition in Higher education where the professionals and leaders of many countries of the old British Empire were educated in Britain. These high fees have not only reduced the influence which British education had in the world, they have also diminished the rich cultural mix that is an important element of any university. I completed successfully my Post-graduate and Post-doctoral studies in Edinburgh and started my research career as a grain scientist at a research institute in Surrey, England, in 1968.

For unknown reasons providence has enabled me to avoid or manage the malice and nonsense of racists. In this regard, a minor incident comes to mind. In 1971, I was invited to an International Conference in Portugal to present a piece of my research work. The work described an invention in grain processing which was in use in the industry. I returned to Heathrow (London) with a group of British colleagues. My colleagues passed easily through Immigration. I was told to wait. The young officer was not convinced that I was with the group. After a difficult debate with the young man, my boss, Dr A H Cook FRS approached us and said, "Do what you must, Palmer but remember that logic is wasted on the illogical." The officer retreated and stamped my passport. On the coach I opened my passport and noticed that he had stamped… 'Visitor for 3 months'. Such incidents can occur at any time and black people have had to learn to live with unpredictable abuse. However, such incidents serve the useful purpose of illustrating the general state of thinking of sections of the community. There is little doubt that ignorance is a major factor in racism and that education and common respect in the community can limit the damaging effects of this disease.

The negative perception of the 'Black Outsider' is still prevalent in our society. For example, recently, I was in the reception area of a large legal institution to attend a meeting. I asked the receptionist to inform the person that I had come to see that I had arrived. After some considerable time my colleague came to the reception area to collect me. He then told me that when he asked the receptionist if Professor Palmer had arrived, he was told, "No, Professor Palmer has not yet arrived…but there is some black guy waiting to see you!" Another irritating but equally silly encounter occurred recently on a train to London where I was asked to give a lecture on education and race. A man grabbed my arm complaining about seat reservations. Before I could respond his friend whispered in his ear, "John, John, he is not the bloody porter!"

To recount all such encounters would be a waste of time. However, each encounter helps to illustrate the complexity of the racial attitudes that infect our society. For example, some time ago, on my return from promoting my institution abroad I was informed that my white colleagues had held a meeting against me. When I asked one of them why he had been involved in this he replied, "What could I do, I was up for promotion?" What disappointed me most was that not one of these 'educated' people said, "This is wrong, I want no part in it." In another similar incident the only comment from a white colleague was, "How the hell do you put up with things like that?" My response was, "With the best weapon allowed... *education!*"

That people like myself should require the help of 'Good Samaritans' to achieve what they could have achieved on their own is a sad indication of the damage that small, mean-minded people do to our institutions. Institutions are not racist, people are. Such people neither respect the law nor the concept of Britishness. To them race laws are political palliatives that can be ignored and Britishness only applies to white people. To make lasting progress, the 'good people' of the system should let racists, of any kind, know that the evil they practice will not be tolerated.

Of the numerous concerns we had as British Subjects, the greatest ones were that many 'good people' said that racist politicians such as Powell and Nabarro were right, and that our *Mother Country and Church were silent.* In response to these disappointments we formed prayer meetings and we danced, when we could, to the music of our Sound Systems. Our jobs paid our way, but we were sustained by our prayers, music and a historical sense of belonging... all products of our African-British (Jamaican) heritage. We called each other *Brother-man* and *Sister Chile,* to re-assure each other because we knew that where there is no sense of belonging damaged lives are found. To sideline community crimes as 'black-on-black' or 'Afro-Caribbean' crimes is unwise, because such narrow views divide the community further along insoluble racial lines. *Punish the guilty, not the people.* From any quarter, punish those who prey on others because it is easy. Racial differences or difficulties are not excuses for criminality.

Stereotyping increases prejudice. For example, the term 'Afro-Caribbean' is not equivalent to 'Afro-American'. In the media, it depicts negative skin colour rather than nationality and should be removed from serious useage. We must not approve inappropriate labels that undermine our nationalities and black identity (see articles 13,14 and Epilogue). Thankfully, the tendency for human beings to use skin colour to erect social barriers is often matched by the capacities of human beings to transcend such prejudice. A few years ago I arrived at Harwich to board a ferryboat to Holland to give a lecture on barley and malt. As I left the crowded train, I realised that I had left my passport in Edinburgh. The port official told me that I would not be allowed to travel. Just as I was about to leave, a chanting came from the crowd behind me: "Let him on, let him on, let him on." I turned and noticed that the chanting came from a host of young men wearing green and white scarves...they were Celtic Football Supporters. The police and the port officials formed a circle to discuss the matter. To my astonishment I was given a temporary travel document. It was not until the crowd of young men had hoisted me onto the boat and into the bar that I realised the reason for their protest. They had mistaken me for a Celtic Football Supporter...I was wearing a green velvet jacket! Somehow, this football encounter has contributed to my belief that humanity has the compassion to transcend the damaging social barriers that wicked people have constructed from skin colour. Although this gesture of support may merely reflect the importance of common identity in group behaviour, improvements in human relationships depend on the goodness that motivates people to defend the rights of others. It has often worried me why, so few people, took so long, before they agreed that New World slavery was wrong...

I was about ten years old when Reverend died and I was in the 'big-children' part of the Church School. Singing and scripture were the main subjects. Punishment for misbehaving during these lessons was severe. The beating strap was made of leather and had five fingers and, like our spoons and trains, was *Made in Britain*. Curiously we were proud of this branding and believed it to be the best. Reverend Nichols told us many stories from the Bible. He also told us that there was slavery in Jamaica and at one time Jamaica had many thousands of slaves... many thousands more than were present in America. I used to ask him, "What was slavery?" He always gave the same answer, "Slavery was a long and cruel silence and a bad mistake...my mistake." "How did that mistake happen?" I would ask, and he always gave the same answer, "No one knows, but mistakes happen and they may be God's way of showing people that cruelty is not only wrong, it produces terrible consequences."

This puzzled me and I started to dream about New World slavery and how the Reverend and I fitted into this human tragedy...a tragedy that has been underestimated with regard to its cruelty and denied with regard to its terrible consequences, then and now. A tragedy that has produced lynching, social isolation, poverty and abuse. However, to black people, the only thing worse than this tragedy is its denial.

Today I am very much older and childhood dreams have turned

into sad and happy experiences. Thankfully, we can be changed by education. As a boy in London, I was asked the time by a white neighbour who believed that black people were backward. "What's the time, little African?" he asked mockingly, pointing to the sun. I looked towards the sun and said, "Ten minutes past three." Covertly, he looked at his watch and confirmed that my time was correct! Many weeks later we passed each other in the street. We both nodded and he muttered the apology, "Good on you, son!"

About forty five years later, as an adult in Edinburgh, two little boys followed me around a paper shop for a while pointing at me, the younger boy said, "Look, there is a nigger." The older boy slapped him on the head and said, "It is rude to point..." Surely, if white children can be taught not to point at adults, they can be taught not to call them niggers - racism is learnt not inherited.

Ignorance and prejudice produce nasty people that mock and abuse other people because of differences in colour and culture. Without doubt, we have all been damaged by the holocaust of New World slavery, for we all know the negative images of black people that have come from that evil event. Without question, we are bound together forever in this historical marriage which cannot be dissolved and therefore must succeed. These may seem hard truths to swallow, but then, historical truths only offend the unjust, who peddle hate, unfairness and division in the community.

In *The Enlightenment Abolished narrative* (page 58) there are no tables or figures to show profit from slavery or the high price of slaves. There are no reproductions of *Run Away* notices depicting shackled humans either on ancient ships or in strange fields reaping sugar cane, coffee, corn, cotton, tobacco or spices, for 'masters' with whips and guns. We have seen these terrible images many times and it is worrying that many people are becoming inured to them and that some people have used them, without respect, to even 'adorn' commercial wallpaper. However, despite the historical importance of these images one question must be…do they convey the *tragic consequences* of slavery? Despite the historical importance of these images they essentially incite emotion. However, what is needed is an insight into life and death during our slavery and how they affect us all today.

The legacies of our slavery are various and difficult to define. Unlike other human tragedies its wickedness is made worse by the ignorance that denies a shared history. It is unfortunate that New World slavery has contributed to what racists regard as, 'earned cultural rights' to castigate others debilitated and put in doubt by the same historical circumstances. However, no living person has personally 'earned' culture and citizenship. These are bestowed by accidents of history, birth or by the law. Therefore, it is misguided for anyone to boast about the legacy of a terrible crime that still offends.

Recently, it has been proposed that multiculturalism is a limitation to the development of Britishness and should be discontinued as a concept. This is incorrect. Multiculturalism teaches social co-existence: Britishness embodies political belonging. Both concepts complement each other to produce citizens with equal rights and responsibilities. The greatest limitation to the development of citizenship is not muticulturalism, it is the word race. It is divisive in every context in which it is used and should be abolished. For example the words *race relations* should be replaced by the words *human relations*. Citizenship is more important than which team one cheers for in sport. Citizenship is a sense of belonging that comes from the feeling that rights are equal and that the system is fair and accessible. Without a sense of belonging even good people can turn into monsters. Incidentally, many Scottish and Welsh people do not cheer for England in sport but are not disloyal to the country… If multiculturalism is to continue to have a positive role in society, the contributions made by all the people of the British Empire to Britishness should be taught and admired. Without admiration there can be no resolution to racial prejudice.

Dispite political footwork to appease culture-phobics, the concept of *Diversity* is *Multiculturalism* by another name. If words such as diversity and ethnic (minority) are used mainly with regard to non-white people, they will take on the connotation of 'Outsiders' and lose their purpose and universality of meaning. The sameness of humanity is greater than its differences. That I was asked if I would change the title of a lecture on 'Ethnic Foods' to 'Foods from Afar' indicates how people avoid facing important issues by spurious changing of words.

Irrespective of skin colour: those with their copied arrogance and smugness should become tolerant and fair: those with their doubts and fears should not react by damaging themselves or, through their actions, confirm negative stereotypes that diminish other people. In many ways, what we are reflects the pride of past victories and the humiliations of past defeats. This should not be overlooked if we are to understand each other. For some to dismiss the concerns of others as, 'chip on the shoulder' or 'thin skin', is disgraceful.

One dangerous consequence that has come from the word race is that some people, have tried, unsuccessfully, to turn social differences into genetic differences. This is the 'proof' racists need to justify the nonsense that skin colour and the shape and form of human beings indicate differences in intelligence and worth. The racist concepts of intelligence that have been drawn from the book, *The Bell Curve* or from the work of Eysenck and Jensen are scientifically worthless because they were derived from surveys which had no controls. In addition, those 'researchers' that have been involved in this kind of puerile racial propaganda, have never understood the relevance of scientific control. Without proper controls, research results are meaningless. In this regard, a proper control group, to any black group descended from slaves, should be whites that have been subjected to black enslavement for over 400 years. Since this concept is unthinkable, research that tries to show that social differences between black and white people are of genetic origins should be disregarded because historical and demographic differences render such comparisons unscientific. It is nonsense to compare the academic performance of under-privileged children with those of privileged children of any ethnic group. Such kinds of dangerous propaganda masquerading as science would not be tolerated in any other area of scientific research.

The neglect and indifference shown by many learned institutions to education and race, as a serious subject of study, has contributed to the damaging perception that 'race relations' is criminal activity associated with the police and black people. In this regard, the war against racism should not only be waged against those in the police who are racists, it should also be waged, with equal rage, against others engaged in the foul practise of racism.

New World slavery was never peaceful and there were many moments of human defiance. Two come to mind. One such moment was in 1760 when a Jamaican slave, who was being *slow-burned* for 'impudence' threw a burning log from the fire that consumed him, at his 'owner' and executioner. The other was in 1782 when Admiral Rodney, with 36 British ships against 34 superior French and Spanish ships, won the Battle of the Glorious 12th of April in the Caribbean, to keep Jamaica and other Caribbean islands, British. Even as slaves we fought for Britain against the French. Then we were more important than kith and kin in the American colonies but now, all we want are our human rights so that we can compete equally. Robert Burns, who was fond of Jamaica and knew its value to the British Empire, was not a man to waste words on what was not relevant to the human condition. He toasted the victory of Rodney thus: "Here's to the Memory of those on the Twelfth we lost! We lost, did I say? No, by Heaven that we found! For their fame it shall live while the world goes round…" This victory secured Britain's dominance and wealth in the Caribbean and paved the way for Nelson's victory at Trafalgar, 23 years later. In my dream we are all in the fire and on Rodney's ships and share the same defiance of the enemy. It should be noted that the defiance of the unknown Jamaican slave that was murdered by burning was of the same heroic kind as that of Leonidas of Ancient Greece.

There are some who believe that Britishness is an unpalatable legacy of the past and should be forgotten and replaced. But how can we replace history? Among other things, history reminds us of the contributions and rights of the people that make up the communities of the world. Like many of the people of Jamaica, my Mother was proud of her country's contribution and connection to Britishness. This Britishness belongs equally to those who were slaves and those who were masters. She was proud and pleased that I would go to Buckingham Palace to receive an OBE from the Queen for my contribution to grain science. She told everyone in the hospital. Sadly, after 56 years in Britain she died on the 9th of December, 2003, the day before I received the award. Before she died she reminded me that the award was a symbol not bad money. To reject such a collective award one would need the permission of all those who have contributed to the award. My Mother also added that anyone who is a product of Britishness and advocates abolition of this award does not understand that history affects us all differently. To change the name of the award would be humbug because all British awards, irrespective of name, reflect the same system. She was also suspicious of the motives of those who turn down an award in public when it could have been refused in private. Values are not made or changed by awards.

After I accepted the OBE award at the Palace, London, a band played melodic music in the large red-carpeted room. Amid the splendour, I could see ancestors slaving in ripe cane and coffee fields hoping that their hopes would be fulfilled. The award is their achievement, not mine. After the award ceremony I was congratulated by a stranger from Edinburgh, who asked, "Are you a member of the society?" Not being sure of 'the society' to which he referred, I replied, "Not yet, but now it matters even less!"

Together: Africa, The British Empire, Jamaica, New World Slavery and Britain make up our historical story. This story cannot be changed to suit the sensibilities of those who do not like parts of the whole. The entire story remains to be told to help improve community relationships because, for example, in a recent discussion of Britishness, very few people knew that the 'red areas' on an old map of the world depicted the British Empire; some thought the red areas were, "where it was hot"! At its simplest, our story says...we have a right to be here, in Britain.

Providentially, Reverend Nichols' 'mistake' of New World slavery has joined us together forever and cannot be dismissed by racial prejudice and the merciless self-interest shown by slave master William Adlam (1820) and his kind *(see Letter Home, p46)*. The enlightened comments and decree by Lord McEwan, in an Edinburgh court (May 2002), not only highlighted the wrongs of racism in a moral, lawful and therefore rightful society; they were also timely warnings to 'closet racists' and 'racists at large', as well as a severe punishment for a terrible crime against an ethnic person.

Racism is anti-creation, anti-country and illegal. That we have to imprison racists is regrettable. However, it is evident that some people derive status, power and pleasure from harming others, by 'sword or word'. It is sad that the law remains a primary defence against racism. In institutions, breaking of racial laws will not be excused by dismissive phrases such as, 'canteen culture', 'isolated case', 'indifference to race laws' or by the 'bad apple' analogy. Citizenship cannot be complete if rights, responsibilities and feelings of belonging are undermined by injustices such as racism.

Now, those who see the current concept of 'Institutional Racism' as a panacea, should note that racists in institutions, unlike racists on the street, tend to be 'closet racists' and are difficult to detect. They are masters of the racial aside which indicates personal problems of low esteem. The unfair job-selection policy of one such person was to turn down all candidates, if any candidate was of ethnic minority origin. This unacceptable practice not only denied jobs to qualified ethnic minority people, it prevented complaints of racism and circumvented the law. In a society where education fails to prevent or cure racism, the law cannot afford to fail. Institutions which have good race relations practice should be accredited to help remove backward indifference to the law.

It is baffling why even well-meaning people cannot understand that attempts to redress and remove colour prejudice are not special treatments, and that true equality will not be achieved until racist attitudes and ideologies that debilitate non-white people are banished from what we think and do. A white skin colour should not confer social advantages. A non-white skin colour is neither a disability nor an indicator of low potential. A short conversation overheard on a tube train may help to illustrate the importance of skin colour and prejudice in our society. Some time ago I boarded a tube train at Turnpike Lane in London after visiting my Mother who was very ill. Two old white men had just started a new topic in their conversation. "Herbie, whatever happened to your son?" "Ah, he went to Cambridge." "And did you ever change his name, Herbie?" "No, we never bothered because he got into a good law firm and now he is a judge, his foreign name doesn't matter anymore." Both men nodded, they were *system conscious*. For them, colour was not an issue but a foreign name was perceived to be a problem...a problem that could be managed by changing a name. Sadly, colour prejudice does not lend itself to such simple solutions. Fundamentally, skin colour is the important organ of the diversity of the Human Race, and its dishonouring by colour prejudice is mindless, irrational and unacceptable in a fair and just society. That colour (race) prejudice had to be made a crime to reduce the terrible abuse of non-white people, is one of the great tragedies of human history. It is not clear why we should have come to this but such tragedies tell us that although nature's future cannot be predicted, we can predict, to some degree, the consequences of the good or evil that we do.

System consciousness is an important feature of the education we require to live in any community. It is an essential component of citizenship. As a concept, it is easier to describe than define. For example it is that knowledge, which makes us aware that it is far wiser to leap into the dark with a torch than without!

System conscious education begins in the home and develops during schooling. Failure in this area of education limits the development of attitudes and skills required by individuals to respond appropriately to meet the interests of self and society which are important features of citizenship. Rules are essential ingredients of citizenship. System conscious education helps us to know and respect the rules. It also helps us to *play the game*. Role models have been proposed as an important learning strategy for children who have educational difficulties. Role models usually encourage imitation of life style, they are not substitutes for the education and skills required to meet social expectations. In the absence of effective strategies which promote educational development in different communities, the influence of the role model concept on poor-achievers is simplistic and is likely to be of limited educational value. The support of parents and teachers are the best role models for children.

System conscious education promotes social mobility and develops social potential. Social mobility enhances freedom and social potential allows opportunities to be taken. Therefore, any policy designed to develop learning and skills should include all aspects of system consciousness that help individuals to access the system and defend themselves against racist individuals and institutions. Effective control of racism in an institution is not about the role an ethnic minority person may play in that institution, it is often about the winks and nods and the illegal acts of group-cultures that deny rights and undermine fairness in institutions. Therefore, it is unlikely that institutional racism will be solved by faster promotions or better representation because it reflects historical prejudices, learnt in childhood, that defy decency and the law, and are difficult to change. The long term solution lies not with the stick of the 'race relations industry' but with the carrot of a balanced education at school.

Photo Gallery

FIGURES

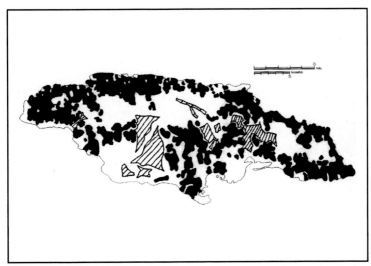

Map of Jamaica: Black areas represent sites of cane sugar production, hatched areas represent coffee-growing areas (about 1805). In 1805 sugar production in Jamaica was worth about £600,000,000 to Britain ...in today's money (Api production, Jamaica, 1975). Slave population ca. 300,000...ca. £100 per 'best' slave.

Plantation in Jamaica: Slaves returning to the estate after a full day growing sugar cane and coffee (Hakwell, 1820).

Oakton Colonial House: In St. Andrews, Jamaica. Similar in design to East Street Colonial House, Kingston, Jamaica (1986).

IMPRESSION OF EAST STREET COLONIAL (WOODEN-BRICK) HOUSE, JAMAICA

My Grandaunt: Auntie, on Sunday standing outside her Church, with her Bible (1958).

Aunt Mina, after Church (1935): Taken downtown (Orange Street) by Mr Morais.

My Grandaunt: Auntie, standing in our backyard at John Street, Allman Town, Jamaica (1958).

My Mother, brother and I in 1944, on Sunday after Church.
Photo taken downtown (Orange Street) By Morais, a local photographer.

Side entrance to North Street Congregational Church, Jamaica - now called North Street United Church (built in 1837).

At my Aunts' house (post Allman Town) in Jamaica, after Church. From left to right: Aunt Hilda, Uncle Ferdy, Aunt Laura in 1986.

At the side door of North Street Church, leading to my school and Princess Street (1986). From right, Aunt Kate and my cousin Liz. To my left Miss Rob (Robinson) my primary school headmistress.

My Mother is given flowers of appreciation by Mrs Mavis Stewart MBE (left) of the Association of Jamaicans in 2002.

Receiving a local carving from Mr Michael Karanja, Chief Executive of Kenya Breweries, for helping educational development in grain science in Kenya 1995.

Teaching and representing Britain during a export trade visit to China, 1999.

Professor Palmer: Chairman of the Scottish Section of The Institute of Brewing. Brewing and Distilling Conference, Aviemore 1991.

Professor Palmer: Showing British barley to overseas visitors at Heriot-Watt University, Edinburgh, Scotland. He has published extensively on Grain Science and was invited to write the foreword of the current *Encyclopedia on Grain Science (2004)*.

Articles Published

by the author on Education, Britishness
and Citizenship, between 1969 and 2007,
as part of his voluntary work

WHERE CHILDREN STILL ARE SEEN AND NOT HEARD by Geoff Palmer

Published in the Times Educational Supplement, 20.3.70 to extend an earlier publication in the same Journal (15.8.1969), that ignorance of British West Indian culture is a major reason why many West Indian children fail in the educational system.

In Jamaica, children like myself started school at about seven years of age. The school would invariably be church-tied: the teachers were mighty and the British clergy all-mighty. The repetitive terror of the three Rs was only broken by long singing periods and compulsory Friday morning services in the adjoining church.

There I "singed" and I "songed" until I heard that my mother had scraped together enough money for me to join her in England. When I left Jamaica at the advanced age of 14 my education had progressed from my two-times to my 12-times table while my singing had rocketed from Three Blind Mice and Yes, Jesus Loves Me to the illustrious but mysterious heights of The Magnificat, Psalm 232, Who is Sylvia?, Row Boys Row, and Loch Lomond.

Having only ever done arithmetic, to be asked at the end of an 11-day journey covering 5,000 miles to tackle rows of figures under the strange heading of "mathematics" was a paralysing encounter; after many failed tests I finally made it to Shelburne Road Secondary Modern School.

At school the behaviour of the teachers was rather perplexing at times. Lack of effort met with no verbal or physical retribution

- the teacher merely passed on to the next boy. If there was any reading to be done, the teacher did it and there was also the additional luxury of no homework. To my relatives this was sheer folly but to me the teacher was like a kind relative.

In such a situation, one can easily see how a West Indian child can be inadvertently "passed over" academically. The apparent "softness" of the teacher is an ideal climate for the adjustment of the perplexed child. However, there are counter-pressures from the home, up to four hours' homework per day, and a parent might well find additional chores for a child who has no homework, as a deterrent against "laziness".

With continued criticism from home about his "dunceness", a child may become suspicious of his teacher, suspecting a deceitful plot to impede his academic progress. The teacher, often ignorant of the child's cultural and home experiences, may attribute the child's behaviour to maladjustment, low intelligence and language deficiencies.

Superimposed on this home-school conflict the child has the additional anxiety of being told that he doesn't speak English. Unlike the educated West Indian who knows the difference between Plantation English and Standard English, the West Indian immigrant cannot always see the difference. He becomes insecure and hurt when it is suggested that he doesn't speak English. His immediate reaction is one of confusion, suspicion and aggression to a statement which, if true, deprives him of the feeling of belonging that a language confers.

In schools where immigrant children are allowed to drift in increasing confusion, alarming and dangerous conclusions may be drawn from their performance of standard IQ tests. When I arrived in England I was slow to appreciate the purpose of "play bricks" and the different pronunciation of identical words often rendered them meaningless.

In difficult areas where local authorities have instituted good parent-school relations, pre-school centres, adequate primary schools and remedial language classes, West Indian children do as well as their English peers who also benefited from the improved facilities.

But some local educational authorities seem to have been somewhat slow to assist West Indian children and these unfortunate children must make, unassisted, the necessary adjustments between two deceptively similar cultures. It may be infinitely more difficult for a Jamaican child to unlearn Plantation English, with its deceptive similarities to Standard English, than for a Greek Cypriot child to grasp the differences between Greek and Standard English.

Often some parents don't help. The Jamaican immigrant philosophically accepts his low status and attributes it to a system which did not provide the educational opportunities he needed to be "somebody". He is therefore very concerned about the educational future of his children. Punishment in the Jamaican home is derived from British (Victorian) culture. A "smack" may be referred to as a "beating". A smack is associated with discipline, and should not be mistaken for abuse.

But with all their concern, many parents are now aware that some of their transferred cultural beliefs may be working against the academic performance of their children. For example, West Indian parents will buy large expensive encyclopaedias for their children, while refusing to buy more attractive annuals and popular readers, which they dismiss as "rubbish books". Curiosity is not always tolerated and an over-curious child may be punished for being "too inquisitive". The Victorian maxim that a child is supposed to be "seen and not heard" is still upheld. Play in the garden can be accepted but play in the house is often interpreted as "bone idleness" and chores are provided to correct this.

Fathers are too work-weary to take their sons on excursions; none the less there is strong resentment towards boys being part of an outside group or club, which many parents feel is the path to lawlessness. A child might have accepted this attitude in Jamaica, but seeing the activities of other children in England, the Jamaican child becomes resentful of its parents' apparent lack of interest in them. Some parents whom I have met complained that while teachers are prepared to provide running shoes and football boots for their children, they are not interested in giving them homework.

As a result of unfulfilled educational aspirations conflicts between parents and children tend to increase rather than die down after the child has left school. Some West Indian parents still consider children as a form of material and emotional insurance; any attempt of the child to assert itself as an independent working unit meets with strong disapproval, and interpreted as gross disobedience and ingratitude.

Continual nagging may drive a boy from his home and from the future security of his apprenticeship to the immediate monetary rewards of the factory. But boredom soon leads to irregular working habits, and eventually the boy joins a group of youths with similar frustrations. Confrontation with the law is the next step.

I once stood with a boy's mother in court and heard the magistrate deny legal aid on the grounds that "you coloured people have too many cars and houses". The boy comes to believe that he and his friends are the victims of white persecution, guiltless of any anti-social behaviour. At this stage institutional correction, just or unjust, is taken casually as confirmation of white prejudice.

For the sake of home and society, local education authorities youth employment officers and employers must make every effort to ensure that genuine ability in West Indian children is not overlooked. On the other hand teachers should be wary of making unrealistic promises about the child's future abilities merely to calm down anxious West Indian parents. This kind of thing only arouses parental hostility, both to the system and the child, when it leaves school without scholastic attainment.

If we are to prevent racism we must give political and financial support to people best qualified to teach and guide all young people. In the long run, only harm can come of a situation where immigration officers, local politicians and semi-officials continue to consider themselves experts on human behaviour and learning.

HANDSWORTH: CARIBBEAN BLACK COUNTRY
by Geoff Palmer

Published in the Times Educational Supplement, 16.6.72 to highlight some of the social complexities inherent in a British West Indian community.

If Brixton is little Jamaica then Handsworth, in Birmingham, is little Kingston. Direct Food Supplies of Soho Road does not sell Hovis: it sells hard-doe buns, sweet cup, goat, fish, skellion, pimento, grater (coconut) cake, cut (coconut) cake, renta yam, yellow yam, coco, ochra, green bananas, goat chops, garden eggs, chocho and bay rum. Behind the large plate-glass window, the Jamaican owner chops corned pig tails.

On the other side of the road is *The Elite*, an Asian shop. The window is decorated with rows of flaccid plucked chickens and unfamiliar little yellow balls. Then there are bird peppers, sweet potatoes, bags of corn meal, Oxford encyclopaedias and stocks of sugar cane, and bags of Joe Lyons fair cakes. A Jamaican woman enters the Asian shop and asks for a packet of Brooke Bond tea..."Just as good." "Not that tea," she says, "it's no damn good, my boy reckons that's the monkey tea!"

I follow her toward Thornhill Road. She goes into another Asian shop and I walk up Thornhill Road and enter (uninvited and unexpected) to the police station, which, according to the Handsworth report by Agustus John, "is one of the buildings most dreaded and most hated by black Handsworth". The building, which has obviously seen better days, is no more imposing than the Jamaican-occupied houses down the road. Indeed, the Rentokil quarters in nearby Grove Lane look the most prosperous in the immediate vicinity.

The hallway of the station is small, dull and quiet. To the right is the interview room and to the left a glass partition with a small "conversation" window. A white woman holds the hand of a dark child, reports the disappearance of a purse and leaves. A Jamaican speaks in hushed tones about family matters. I tell the PC at the window that I would like to talk to someone who is involved with immigrants. He says that Sergeant Bradley, the CRC officer, is out, but will be back at 1pm.

I return at 1pm and am led into the interview room by Sergeant Bradley and another policeman who introduced himself as Bill. "I make frequent visits to the schools to answer questions about the attitudes of policemen to immigrants in Handsworth. Questions are invariably about police harassment, but it's usually about what their friends have told them," the CRC officer tells me. "Most of the kids have never been in trouble, and although the sessions are heated I am usually well received."

He maintains that as much as 60 per cent of the problems in which the police become embroiled are not really police matters and that there would be less ill-feeling in Handsworth if they were dealt with by qualified social bodies. "The schools should be involved in this aspect of community education because while English parents listen, most West Indian parents don't." But he believes that things are improving.

"For example, the Handsworth Community Venture has bought a house to be run by a Jamaican, Mr. Vic Fennell, as an Advice Centre to prevent parents bringing their children to the station for advice. He explained the sensitivity of his job carefully, "You see, you raise your voice in anger because you're tired and the kid starts to manufacture hate and we're all in trouble".

PC Bill is an impassive Black Country man and has been a Handsworth policeman for 22 years. "Listen son, I know this area well. It was nice once...kippers and curtains...but it isn't now. It's not the immigrants' fault. The area has got old. Troublemakers come here and spend a few days and go away and tell a load of lies. I know more Jamaican parents than Gus John could ever dream of knowing. I visit their homes; I talk with them; they give me tea. Their boy misbehaves in the home: they say to him..."You do that again and out you go, boy." He does it again and there's no joking...out he goes. They complain to me that they throw their children out because of us, the police. I ask them: "How is this?" They say: "Back home we could give them a good hiding but here they threaten to put you, the police, on us. This has happened and it worries me because these are the kids the Black Power troublemakers are after."

He goes on: "There are no organized gangs in Handsworth. Jamaicans don't form gangs; they don't like rules and regulations. For example, there's a reggae party down the road and you tell them to turn down the noise as it's late and a neighbour has made a complaint: they'll suck their teeth and just ignore you...not because they want a fight but because they reckon that a 'little noise' isn't a crime. But we have to push the issue of the noise-complaint and in the end we have to arrest somebody.

"The responsible blacks who have lived a long time in Handsworth have come to terms with our way of life and are very conservative now. You tell me, where was Gus John when some of his friends picketed the station four weeks ago? Only 23 people arrived - out of a black community of thousands.

"You read about gangs in Handsworth and wrongful arrest...the kids that make trouble think they are right and we think they are wrong: mistakes happen but there's no organized law-breaking in Handsworth. The closest we got to an organized event was the abortive hot-air punch-up which was supposed to take place between the Handsworth Boys School (mostly black) and the Handsworth Grammar (mostly white) in Handsworth Park. We are not trained social workers, we are law-enforcement officers who have had to take on other duties which no one wants to do."

I leave the station with the intention of visiting some of the Jamaican-run pubs; of finding out more about the demonstration at the station and about some of the problems of black youth in Handsworth.

The Jamaican-run pubs in Handsworth are home from home institutions. After work the Jamaican men make their way to the pub to chat, drink beer and listen to non-stop reggae music. In the pub I visit the walls are lined with platted straw and bamboo. There is a composite picture of Jamaican scenery, a picture of John and Robert Kennedy with Martin Luther King between them and two African masks which the man beside me describes as, "being made right here in Birmingham". The publican is a shrewd Jamaican ex-serviceman who sees trouble before it starts.

"Nice brotherman, cool it", is sufficient. As in the other Jamaican-run pubs or in clubs like the Beverly, his family helps behind the bar and they all wear a "Welcome" badge.

It is difficult not being a Jamaican in a Jamaican pub because the conversation invariably comes round to..."You remember Race Course"...or..."One night I was walking through Jones Town".

There are two Indian records to fifty Reggae or Tamla Motown records on the juke box but the Indians don't seem to mind. In another Jamaican-run pub down Soho Road, Jamaicans are seated in the Jamaica room and Indians are in the India room.

During a visit to the urinals a turbaned Indian tells me of the occasion he was on a bus in the city and a nice white woman asked him if he liked it in the city and how she was for integration and understanding of the races and when she got up to leave the bus she bade him goodbye and wished that his head would get better soon.   We both laugh and he goes back in the India room and I go to the Jamaica room to join my friend who tells me we have been invited to a party. Just as we are about to leave PC Bill and Sergeant Bradley come in and say hello to some of the Jamaicans and buy drinks: whether they are loved or not they are definitely not strangers in Handsworth.

A Jamaican birthday party in Handsworth is no different from the same event in London. The host is a tough beefy Jamaican and he is in charge of arrangements for his party. He lights the candles on the cake and says "his few words" and closes with a general rendering of the Lord's prayer. We all sing happy birthday to the well-dressed Jamaican girl at the end of the table and she blows out the candles and thanks us in a strong Birmingham accent.

The table is moved into the kitchen and the music starts again. After many whiskies and glasses of nutrament (an egg-flip-like drink designed for the Jamaican market), curry goat and pork, the guests drift away.

A small group sits and begins to talk. The host, who had recent business with the law, says: "I don't trust the British police… mind you I didn't trust the Jamaican ones either. As a black man I must sympathize with any black movement but although my association, WINA (West Indian National Association), asks all shades of militants to speak to us we do not let them interfere with our club. We have our own committee. We buy flats, put them right and let them cheaply to our people."

He explains: "The march on Thornhill Road police station against blatant police harassment failed because we were let down by immigrants who beforehand had pledged their support. Black people just don't want to be seen demonstrating outside the police station…they are afraid of victimization." "Afraid!" exclaimed another member of the group, "I'm not afraid, I have to go to work to pay my mortgage. Listen brother, why not get a lawyer to help fight your cause?"

Roy Pitters is a Jamaican youth worker and has lived in Birmingham for 23 years. Having heard his name mentioned in a conversation, I rang him and an hour later I was in his sittingroom. On the wall are two certificates, one of the National Association of Youth Clubs and the other The City of Birmingham Joint Training Committee for Youth Workers. "Up until 1967 there were only two black youth workers in Birmingham - much less Handsworth", he says, and adds that, "At that time many of our Jamaican youths carried knives and this resulted in the accidental stabbing of a youth in Handsworth Park. In the so-called Handsworth Report, Gus John intimates that because I stood outside youth clubs and begged my Jamaican boys to hand over their knives before entering, I betrayed them and am one of the most resented men in Handsworth today.

"Such nonsense doesn't worry me because while I was in Birmingham facing the knives and meeting church leaders and police officers in this front room about the question of my youths, Gus John was either in Grenada or Oxford doing theology. That kid died in my boy's arms and I didn't want any more deaths. It was a time of uncertainty and tension...we couldn't afford the luxury of another Notting Hill in Birmingham. When police brutality is suggested I am the first to protest about it...but I don't try and involve kids in an open confrontation with the police because I regard it as my responsibility to take the matter to the proper authorities which is invariably not the PC on the deck at Thornhill Road. What we want in Handsworth and other immigrant areas are black leaders who will live here and work here, explaining to their brothers the best action to take when difficulties arise...we don't want 5-day residents doing paid surveys.

"I have read that Jamaican kids are useless workers but I am a training instructor for the Amalgamated Power Engineers and if it were Monday I'd show you what the black apprentices can do."

In his report John dismisses current youth work in Handsworth but while I'd be the first to admit that we have a long way to go, some progress has definitely been made: in 1967 there were only two youth clubs for black kids. Today there is the Canterbury Cross with about 300-400 members, Rookery Road Club with 150-200 members, the new Oaklands Youth Centre costing £35,000, with about 300 members, where unemployed youth are attended to by the youth employment officer rather than at the depressing youth employment office. There is also the Newtown Centre at Lozells. The job situation is not rosey, the squeeze is tight in Handsworth and the problems of a black youth who wants to work are cumulative in their final effect.

He gives me a beer. "There are no gangs of black youths in Handsworth...the sooner white people realize that six black kids walking down the road or sitting in the park is not a gang, the better. Jamaicans like to improvise and the peripheral relations they form with each other do not satisfy the rigid rules of a gang group. Like any group they reassure each other when the "intellectuals", the police and their parents, reject them.

"People who 'drop in' on Handsworth don't realize that things like the employment of a full-time social worker at William Murdoch School and the fact that a black boy from that school got into Oxford is a tiny step in the right direction. Equally important is the fact that West Indians travel from Handsworth to Perry Barr to work their allotment, and have made a fantastic job of running many pubs in Handsworth. Blacks don't want patronage, they want an opportunity to explore their new environment.

"We want mothers to stay at home and bring up their children rather than hiving them off to dead-leg babyminders. To achieve this we have to give the immigrant the assurance that he will not be hounded out. Better and cheaper housing, job security, and well-publicized advice centres should provide this assurance. We want our brothers to stop talking and come to live here and help us."

When I arrived at the recently built New Town Centre, the West Indian boys and girls were paying their admission fee to enter what the poster on the door advertises as: New Town Centre Youth Clubs. "It all happens here. 8-14 years...6-8pm, 14-21 years... 7-10.30pm. Activities: Snooker, Table Tennis, Football, Dancing: Thursday, Every Thursday: Reggae - Disco 5p".

"The problem of youth in a deprived area is so vast that it cannot be put into neat academic packages," the warden, Peter Allen, tells me. "West Indians have no inherent sympathy with the way we, the English, do things. For example, the club rules say that the party ends at 10.30pm but they can see no harm in it going on until 1am. So when at first you say "stop" they just say "piss off". One cannot be taught to handle West Indian youth, one merely uses one's eyes and hopes that in time these kids will graduate from calling you: Man, Cock, Bossman, Guv, to *Peter*. This, in itself, is an achievement. To jostle them is an important form of physical contact or else the only contact you have with them is throwing them out. We don't have any Indian teenagers coming here...not formalized enough. However, during the week we have 60 to 70 unemployed Indians who come here to improve their English and to meet."

The West Indian Federation Association Youth Club presents a less optimistic scene. The front door opens on to Winson Green Prison and the inside of the building is in need of decoration. A new telephone lies on a chair. The front room is used for meetings and the large back room for parties. On a chair there is a leaflet calling for action to defeat racialism and unite against police harassment. In the back room an enthusiastic West Indian band, The Explosive Copper Coins band is rehearsing a song called "It's too late to say that you're sorry..." while two Jamaican youths sweep up the bottles, cans and cigarette butts. I asked them about the activities of the club. "The place is a bit rough but we like it here", one of them tells me, "because Mr. Hunt has Black Power ideas we don't get much cash. The police don't bother us much here but if we kids walk in a group and make a bit of noise they are likely to arrest you if you don't do as they say."

Back in Handsworth Park, I ask a Jamaican kid if he knows of any youth clubs in the area. He says, "Yes, the Canterbury Club." I ask him if he goes to the West Indian Federation: he says, "Yes." I ask him why and he says: "Down there, the sound (music) is better." A few steps further in the Park I ask a Jamaican parent what he thinks of the Federation and he says: "I had a decent Christian upbringing and a place in front of a prison is no place for decent kids to go."

If one is to find fault with the good intentions of those who have written about Handsworth (Gus John and John Lambure in The Handsworth Report: Jim Bergman and Bernard Coard in Race Today) attention must be focused on their over-obsession with the police bogy while ignoring the fact that "fluent Swahili" is no substitute for the "detested white-orientated education".

Deprived youth, with no possibility of area mobility, not only require continuity of teaching, but in school they also require continuity and confidence in youth leadership. They need, as Dr. Robert Holman of the Handsworth Adventure Play says, detached youth workers in the Handsworth scene. They want people who will live locally and involve the kids in activities which are beneficial to themselves and the community in which they live. Qualified blacks must go to the "Black Country" to lead.

Postscript 2004: On Saturday the 10th of July 2004 I was given the honour to present the prizes and give a talk on science as a career to the Ishango Science Club Ltd., in Birmingham. The large classroom was full of local black children and their parents. In attendance were volunteer teachers, staff, the Chair – Monica Coke, the Project Manager – Karen Gardiner and Lloyd Blake of the Institute of Jamaica Nationals, Birmingham. This scheme is sponsored by the Birmingham Core Skills Development Partnership and is a successful development, which shows that the difficulties of 1972 were not insurmountable and are being overcome by committed people and institutions. This initiative is a workable model as regards the Science, Engineering and Technology (S. E. T.) scheme, which could be introduced in areas where children need additional educational support.

FOOD FOR THOUGHT IN MULTICULTURAL BRITAIN by Geoff Palmer

Published in the Sunday Express, 25.6.2000 to illustrate that foods from the countries of non-white people (ethnic foods) are an important part of multicultralism in Britain.

Variety is the spice of life, and you need look no further than the haggis for proof of that. For decades, people, inside and outside government have struggled to bring home the concept of a multicultural society. In the Sixties, people talked of New York being a melting pot where the world's nations rubbed shoulders, making it the world's most exciting city.

And maybe the analogy wasn't far wrong for Britain too. Tangerines, tomatoes, chocolate, coffee, sugar, tea, cornflakes, rhubarb, cucumbers, onions, and olive oil, are some of the foods which we in Britain eat every day and are regarded as staples of the British diet. But they are of ethnic origin.

An important feature of any society is that the people in it should have mutual respect for each other's contribution. What more important contribution is there than food? Food which has sustained the people of this society.

The basic mediaeval Scottish diet, although often cited as being healthy, was extremely uninteresting, comprising mainly of soups, purees, beet leaves, cabbage, onions, turnips, leeks and, for the fortunate, salted beef, pork or fish. But that began to change in the 12th century when the package tourists of their day, the Crusaders, brought back sugar from the Middle East.

The history of the British Empire for over three hundred years has been one of securing and maintaining our food supply from the colonies. During the 17th Century, the English fought the Portuguese to secure spices such as cloves, nutmeg and cinnamon to improve the British diet.

Between 1700-1800, the British diet, because of colonisation, had changed dramatically to include tea, coffee, chocolate, potatoes, tomatoes and spices. Economically, and in terms of diet, sugar was regarded as the most important food product by the British. It came primarily from the West Indies colonies. Some of the most important naval battles fought by the British were fought in defence of West Indian islands that had a large Scottish population at the time.

One of the most vital of these was fought against the French in 1782 by Admiral Lord Rodney, which came to be known as the Battle of All Saints or the Battle of the Glorious Twelfth. The significance of this battle can be measured against the fact that the British had "surrendered" to the Americans in 1781, while one of the largest fleets ever put to sea by Britain was off the coast of Florida to fight the French, to protect Jamaica and maintain British dominance in the production of sugar, rum, coffee and spices.

The historical importance of this battle can also be deduced from the knowledge that Rodney had 36 warships and Nelson, at Trafalgar, only had 29. Robert Burns deemed it important enough to write a song about the British victory.

Instead of a song, boys, I'll give you a toast;
Here to the memory of those on the Twelfth we lost;
That we lost, did I say, nay, by heaven that we found,
For their fame it shall last while the world go round.

The benefits of these wars resulted in the development of a supply of cheap food such as sugar, spices, coffee, tea and chocolate from the West Indies and Asia.

Britain's ports grew rich on this trade. Shop owners, such as Thomas Lipton, created the forerunners of our supermarkets. It is curious that our present supermarkets provide one of the few places where the white population is brought into contact with the products of British colonialism without being aware of it. It is also important to note the role, culturally and economically, Indian and Chinese restaurants play in British life.

The Government has emphasised the school curriculum should reflect the multicultural nature of our society. However, there has been little progress. One reason is ignorance of the contribution the colonies have made to this country. It is from this seed of ignorance the monster, racism, continues to grow, spread and divide the human race.

As a Jamaican immigrant who teaches brewing, it gives me pleasure to know Red Stripe and Cobra are among our most successful lagers and they are brewed in the UK by British students whom I have had the privilege to teach.

This is the true nature of the multicultural melting pot. The supermarket shelf is the place where multiculturalism cannot be denied. What has been ignored in the supermarket should become an important part of education.

PUNISHED FOR BEING JAMAICAN by Geoff Palmer

Published in the Edinburgh Evening News, 25.1.03 in response to the visa restrictions imposed on Jamaica in 2003.

Punish the guilty, not the people of Jamaica. Punish the guilty that evade immigration rules, trade in drugs and carry and use guns illegally. But why punish the people of Jamaica for the actions of criminals - some born in Jamaica others born in Britain?

Law-abiding Jamaicans are dismayed that the long 348 years of links between Jamaica and Britain could have been damaged by the actions of people over whom they had no control.

The causes of this criminality are various. Some say that they come from the poverty of Jamaica and the absence of a sense of belonging in Britain. Notwithstanding, the law must be upheld and the people of Jamaica are fully aware of this. That they should have to pay the price of visa restrictions for crimes committed in Britain has damaged the well-being of a proud people that have had to survive on a small, poor island that was, during slavery, the economic jewel in the crown of the British Empire. Kingston Docks in Glasgow and Inveresk Lodge, Inveresk (near Edinburgh) came from this abundance.

During rapid immigration between 1950-1960, Jamaicans worked in jobs that no-one else wanted. These jobs were vital for the post-war recovery of Britain. And most recently, senior nurses have been recruited from Jamaica to help run our hospitals.

However, from the 9th January, 2003, Jamaicans travelling to the UK will require a visa for the first time in nearly 350 years. The governments of Jamaica and Britain have been in negotiations for two years about ways of dealing with the entry of Jamaicans into Britain. Unfortunately, the timing of the British government to impose visa restrictions on Jamaicans has linked the visa issue to the terrible and tragic killing of Charlene Ellis and Latisha Shakespeare in Birmingham on 2nd January, 2003. Jamaicans are distressed by this perception because those involved in this evil crime are likely to have been British citizens, born in Britain. That many people referred to this tragic local crime as a "black-on-black" crime was disgraceful. The racial undertone of this mindless definition is that "black-on-white" crimes and "white-on-white" or "white and black" crimes are more acceptable forms of criminality.

The causes of the Birmingham tragedy are very complex. The crime appears to have been a local act of illegal possession and use of guns. The growing similarity between the use of guns in deprived communities in Britain, like America, reflects the misguided view that guns and knives offer "personal protection" in a violent environment. This kind of social separation tends to exclude the police. In consequence, the support the police needs to solve many local crimes is often withheld. Even community leaders find it difficult to establish lasting social connection with disaffected young people...this is a bio-social problem, not an affliction exported from Jamaica.

That rap music initiates violence is a view based on very little evidence. Beat music has always been associated with current trends in youth violence. The evidence that shows that youth violence is reduced in the absence of beat music does not seem to be available. Until this evidence is available it would be unwise to make such statements which have a ring of anti-black music about them. Jamaican music is a valuable contribution to world music but surely this is hardly a good reason for imposing a visa sanction on its population.

Some of the more serious reasons for imposing visa sanctions on Jamaicans are that six per cent of Jamaican visitors (3,340 people) were refused entry in 2001 and more than 1,000 Jamaicans (mainly children) failed to return to Jamaica in 2002. In 2002, 1,283 Jamaicans were refused entry, a significantly smaller number than the 3,340 of 2001, suggesting that control systems were improving and that the justification of the visa sanction is questionable.

Linked to these immigration issues is the view that many visitors from Jamaica transport drugs to Britain. Although the perception is that Jamaicans are primary transporters of drugs, the Home Office figures published in December, 2002 stated that, of the 40 to 50 tonnes of cocaine shipped to Britain, about 15 per cent came in by air transport worldwide...Jamaica is regrettably a part of this 15%. However, the bulk of the disgracefully large quantity of cocaine that comes into Britain is shipped from various continental countries, many of which have no visa restrictions for entry into Britain.

The vast majority of Jamaicans in Britain are hard-working members of the community and are proud of their long historical links with Britain. First language is an important aspect of culture... the only language of Jamaicans is English, they are treated like social outsiders. At the recent Annual Dinner of the Birmingham based Institute of Jamaican Nationals, that was held at the Aston Villa Football Stadium, I was delighted to have been asked to propose the toast to the Institute and its 555 guests. The event was peaceful and dignified and the Queen was toasted respectfully in the usual manner. An old Jamaican man reminded me after the dinner that Robert Burns' favourite country, after Scotland, was Jamaica. At a meeting of the Leeds Jamaican Association and the London Jamaican Association I encountered the same confidence and Britishness. These aspects of social belonging are sadly missing from the lives of many Jamaican children born in Britain who are descended from black African and white British people yet look only to Africa for identity rather than to Britain, where their heritage through history, name and ancestors is more traceable. Citizenship comes out of a sense of belonging that is based on the belief that social responsibility is the price of equal rights. If rights are not equal or are perceived as not equal, it is difficult to teach social responsibilities. Our history and genes give us a right to be here and this cannot be dismissed or changed by words or deeds from any quarter.

The Home Secretary's view that the imposition of a visa will speed up the passage of "genuine passengers" may indeed be correct. But the possession of a visa will not be a guarantee that the individual carrying it will not have criminal intentions. In fact, the 36 pounds (about 3,600 Jamaican dollars) required for the purchase of the visa and the "expensive" bureaucracy that will be required to secure a visa will increase the percentage of people who may be forced to carry drugs in exchange for a visa.

The main resource left to Jamaicans, after British colonial rule that lasted from 1655 to 1962, is their pride. It is unpardonable that this pride should have been attacked and damaged by the evil actions of those who trade in drugs and guns. The government and the people of Jamaica would never condone such senseless crimes.

It is understandable that the British Government must act to protect law and order in Britain. All Jamaicans understand this position. However, the distress they now endure is the unjust public perception that the visa imposition is linked to the criminal events that took the innocent lives of two promising young ladies on the streets of Birmingham.

However, below the surface of this distress is the optimistic and essentially Christian view that this visa decision will be reversed in the future when it is realized, through education, that the population of Jamaica are not outsiders and not involved in law-breaking in Britain. Jamaicans will work to remove the visa restrictions. At present, they are also working to save their sugar industry from damage proposed by unenlightened sugar policies of the European Commission. Such damage to cane sugar will increase deprivation that started in slavery when Jamaica produced as much as half the world's sugar for Britain. For a small, poor country such as Jamaica to succeed in reducing crimes driven from outside the island, it requires *self-helping* support from Britain to save the residue of a sugar industry that did more than its share to build and sustain an Empire that was British.

EDUCATION, RACE AND CITIZENSHIP
by Geoff Palmer

Written in 2004. Taken from a lecture given at a conference on Citizenship at Edinburgh University, organised by The School of Divinity, Centre for Theology and Public Issues, Edinburgh University, 2003.

Racial tolerance and good citizenship are two of the primary aims of any civilised society. Two institutions to which this important responsibility has been allocated are: Education and the Law. It is therefore evident that if education fails, the law cannot afford to fail. That we, in the United Kingdom have had to pass race relation laws to protect the rights of people of different races, is an indication that education has not managed to convince us that racial prejudice is unfair and wrong. Indeed, the so-called philosophical concepts of an adviser to the Home Secretary propose that, it makes good sense for an employer not to employ black workers if his or her customers will not deal with black people. Such a concept is irrational and absurd in view of the law and the aim to develop good citizenship, where self-interest and greed do not limit rights and justice. However, I still believe that real and lasting improvements in race relations will come from appropriate educational initiatives.

Educational initiatives that work are those which develop admiration and respect for the rights of all the people of our community. Culture embodies customs and practices of different human beings. There is no consistent evidence, that people of different cultures cannot be Citizens of the same community, if a sense of belonging is promoted. The word "race" is divisive and has been used to put people in a social pecking order. Therefore, the continued usage of the word race, when we mean ethnic, reinforces prejudices that state that different races exist.

Our languages and our histories influence our ideologies. For example, there are a large number of people who believe that only white people can be Scottish, English, Irish, Welsh or British. The reason for this belief is difficult to identify but many of our racial prejudices stem from such a view. The word "race" has no clear meaning and carries with it beliefs of social and genetic differences which embody superiority and inferiority. However, the following examples show how the word race can convey differences between people which, on the most superficial examination, do not make sense. We use the words Human Race to convey universal humanity. However, we glibly refer to ourselves as members of, the Scottish race, the English race, the French race or the German race. However, we do not regard a Nigerian as belonging to the Nigerian race or a Kenyan as belonging to the Kenyan race or a Jamaican as belonging to the Jamaican race. Curiously, we tend to regard all black people as belonging to the black race, without having equivalent national and cultural distinctiveness.

The word race exaggerates the importance of skin colour and features but underrates the overriding uniformity of the biological function of humanity. Racism is therefore a product of the human mind...it is based on an evil that deludes but seems right to people who do not know the difference between cultural difference and genetic difference. Indeed, we get some of our fear of the "foreigner" from Gibbons who sold the yarn that if the barbarians can destroy Rome, other foreigners can destroy Britain. Since the British population consists of many foreigners, Gibbons' view does not make sense but this is the essence of racism...what is believed does not make sense.

Hume, our great philosopher, also had a problem with the concept of race. He, with all his mighty intellect, could not accept that because Africans have not built anything like the Castle, they must be inferior to white men. It did not seem to cross Hume's great mind that geography, need and circumstances play a major part in human activity. What is more astonishing than Hume's misunderstanding is that his erroneous view is still held today to the detriment of black people.

One should not be able to turn a "prejudice" into a "fact" but, to justify racism, various scientists have tried to produce evidence that differences in the performance of different "races" in psychology (intelligence) tests are based on genetic differences. The prejudice here is that different races have had different historical experience and no decent researcher would compare the performance of two rats in a test that have had distinctly different histories. Curiously, what would be regarded as unfair and unscientific for rats is regarded as quite suitable for human beings, even though the results of such tests could deny people their due respect and rights.

I see no reason why black or white foreigners cannot be British citizens. White foreigners seem to progress faster in the system than black foreigners. Indeed, many so-called black foreigners, like myself, are long standing members of the British Empire. Jamaica became part of the Empire in 1655 and has derived its language and culture primarily from its Britishness. Many Jamaicans are descended from black and white people. The white ancestors of many Jamaicans are Scottish, many of whom were slave masters. Britishness was a political concept of a world of different people living on the "red areas" of the map of the world. It has nothing to do with colour and race. That to be British...is to be white, is historical nonsense.

After over three hundred years of Britishness, it is problematic that we can subject a Jamaican or any other people of the old British Empire to a British citizen test. There is an inherent injustice in this. That people of the old British Empire should have to pay very high fees to enter our universities does not seem right. That black people, of one of the oldest sections of the British Empire, should be deprived of social rights and be subjected to the indignity of having the right to call themselves black, put out to consultation by civil servants, is an impudent attack on the identity of creation and a large backward step for race relations in Britain. *My colour is me.* It will not be bartered, bought or sold again. Overt racism or the covert racism of the "wink and nod" racist should not be tolerated, from any group or from any quarter.

Recently it has been proposed that multiculturalism is a limitation to the development of Britishness and should be discontinued as a concept. This is incorrect. Multiculturalism teaches social co-existence: Britishness embodies political belonging. Both concepts complement each other to produce citizens with equal rights and responsibilities. The greatest limitation to the development of citizenship is not multiculturalism, it is the word race. It is divisive in every context in which it is used and should be abolished. Citizenship is not about which team one cheers for in sport, it is about a sense of belonging that comes from the feeling that rights are equal. Many Scottish and Welsh people do not cheer for England in sport but are not disloyal to the country...

System consciousness is a term I use to describe one of the important out-comes of education. Without it, it is difficult to function successfully in any society. To produce good citizens, we must not only give people a sense of belonging, we must also ensure that they develop the system consciousness they need to function equally in the society.

FREEDOM COLOUR PREJUDICE
by Geoff Palmer

First appeared in Edinburgh and Lothian Racial Equality Council's Newsletter, December 2006

"My colour is me..." says the poet proudly (Edinburgh and Lothians Racial Equality Council's 35th Anniversary magazine, 2006). Here he tells us that skin colour is a primary part of his slave heritage and freedom: to write it out of documents is a gross insult to natural identity.

The year 2007 will be the 200th anniversary of the abolition of the British Slave Trade. School children to Governments of the United Kingdom are working to commemorate the ending of the purchase/capture and transport of millions of black people, from Africa to areas of the New World such as the West Indies and America.

This short piece is not about the abolition of the slave trade or slavery; it is about the current attempt to remove the word "black" from official documents such as census forms. As a descendant of black Jamaican slaves, I find this intention offensive to my history. I cannot speak for all the descendants of New World slaves but my experience indicates that we honour the skin colour of our slave ancestors and do not want the right to describe ourselves as black taken away by people who do not understand, share or respect our historical experience.

That the eloquence to the biblical phrase, "black but comely", was reworked by racists to create the perception of inferiority and justify enslavement, was a terrible evil. The work of DuBois, Marcus Garvey, Senghor, Biko and others returned the skin colour black to its proper place as a dignified description of a large section of the human race. Out of this work came the renaissance concept of "Black Consciousness"...a concept that has made it possible for a black skin colour to be worn with dignity by anyone that carries the genes of black people. In this regard, black consciousness is about dignity in self, irrespective of the views of others. That anyone would wish to deny the significance of this re-gained dignity of black people reflects ignorance at its worst.

Any attempt to remove the rights of people to describe them as they see themselves is an unacceptable denial of human rights. It is well known that the first step in taking away the freedom of any group of people is the removal of their identity. This pointless attempt to deny me the right to call myself black is an assault on my freedom. I will not accept this. To propose that I should call myself African Jamaican/Caribbean, instead of Black Jamaican/Caribbean is as ridiculous as, one or two Europeans forcing white Americans, whose white ancestors have lived in America for centuries, to call themselves European Americans. Although I respect African people and people who are conveniently black, I will not be a victim of such bad reasoning. In this I expect protection from my government.

Logically, the removal of the colour black, from forms, should also result in the removal of the colour white. Both these changes will require the consent of both races as is clear from the Race Relations Amendment Act 2000. This has not yet been done but must be done to protect the freedom of both races. In addition, the removal of skin colour will make it impossible to monitor racism that is linked to colour. Also, there will be the dangerous deception that, in time, the present significant level of racism towards black people will disappear statistically if the black population is subsumed into a large minority ethnic population. For the sake of peace and progress in our society this must not be allowed to happen.

To try and explain away the word "Black" as an all embracing political concept of "non-whiteness", is unwise, unsound, wrong and disrespectful to black people, descended from a slavery that has been described as "the most profitable evil the world has known". I value the dignity my colour gives me. Racial abuse using the word black will increase if the dignity of the word is slipped under the political carpet. This will cause even greater discomfort to those who do not want to be called black. Such perverse outcomes usually emerge from decisions based on lopsided lobbying and scaremongering, rather than on sound scientific evidence.

Choice is an important part of what we call freedom. That some people do not want to tick skin colour on forms should not deny me the human right of registering my identity as a black person.

THE 200 YEAR COMMEMORATION OF THE ABOLITION OF THE BRITISH SLAVE TRADE IN THE WEST INDIES: 1807-2007

FREEDOM WALK: From Musselburgh High Street to Inveresk Lodge.

The route re-enacts the journey taken by the Jamaican ex-slave Robert Wedderburn in 1795 to see his Scottish father, the ex-slave master James Wedderburn. Robert Wedderburn was born into British slavery in Jamaica in 1762. He was the son of the white slave master, James Wedderburn and a black slave woman, Rosanna.

James Wedderburn, a Scot, went to Jamaica in 1746. He became a notorious slave master and in 1773 returned to Scotland and bought Inveresk Lodge with the money he made, after 27 years in Jamaica, as a slave master. He married well and his Scottish family benefited from his exploits in Jamaica.

In contrast, his slave-son, Robert Wedderburn was forgotten until 1795 when, after gaining his freedom, he travelled from London to Scotland and from Musselburgh to Inveresk Lodge to find his father, James Wedderburn.

James Wedderburn did not allow Robert Wedderburn to enter his house and drove him away with the insulting gift of a "cracked sixpence". Robert Wedderburn (also known as Reverend Robert Wedderburn) returned to London and for the rest of his life, worked as a radical anti-slavery activist. His great rage against chattel slavery in the British West Indies was well known to other abolitionists such as William Wilberforce.

Robert Wedderburn preached and wrote with great force that such slavery was against God, anti-Christian and uncivilised. Thankfully, the British slave trade (abolished 1807) and British slavery (abolished 1834) ended before Robert Wedderburn died in London in 1835.

This commemorative walk of freedom symbolises the hope, the rejection, the hard work and the triumph of a human being who bravely preached that slavery is a grotesque evil that should not be practiced or tolerated by anyone, anywhere.

In 2003, Lord (Professor) Bill Wedderburn (a descendant of Robert Wedderburn) and his wife visited Inveresk Lodge. They visited the house and walked around the beautiful gardens, now owned by the National Trust for Scotland. As we walk through the silence of the garden our thoughts should be on Robert Wedderburn, the ex-slave, who turned his rejection from this house, his father's house, into a quest for freedom...a freedom that brings us together today to celebrate our common humanity.

Material taken from: The Enlightenment Abolished-Citizen of Britishness, Geoff Palmer, Henry Publishing.

The National Trust for Scotland acknowledges the kind permission of Geoff Palmer in allowing us to reproduce this history.

Epilogue

For the future we should talk of one race...the Human race; all one people but different. About the past, we must never forget that 300 years of the most brutal slavery was based on the contrived conclusion that the black colour of the skins of African people made them inferior and ideal material for distant legal enslavement. The consequences of human prejudice are invariably cruel and nothing was crueler than labelling people Chattel and then enslaving them, without a word against the wicked deed, for centuries. The consequences of slavery have made us what we have become...people affected in different ways by the most profitable evil the world has known.

Although we commemorate and learn from other atrocities, there are some who begrudge that the horrors of British slavery, which killed untold millions of defenceless black people, is being remembered in 2007. This slavery was based on skin colour. It has taken more than 200 years for black people to regain the dignity of colour they had before slavery. The source of this dignity-regained was the holocaust of Chattel slavery. From this cultural source flows a lineage from which my black identity is derived. We who are not white share this identity. Any attempt to remove this identity sanctions racism against black people.

Today, 200 years after the abolition of the slave trade, our lineage of being black is: genetic, universal and not controlled by degrees of blackness or laws. In contrast, our links to countries are historical and are affected by degrees of association and laws. Our black identity is an act of creation and cannot be changed by anyone. Therefore, for a group of white civil servants to act on the self-interest and supposed "fear of skin colour abuse" of a handful of Africans and propose replacing black and white categories on census forms with "African" and "European", is imperialistic bias taken too far. This concept of phenotype discrimination is racism by stealth and is saying that, "African" is Negroid-related and "European" is white Caucasian-related. Without a black identity, millions of people, that are neither African-Negro nor Caucasian, would lose their human identity, unity and freedom. "Apartheid purity", Negro or Caucasian, concerns me because at a recent lecture on the heroes of Jamaican slave rebellions, William Gordon, a black Jamaican of mixed race was not mentioned. Bogle, Gordon's companion in nationality, faith, war and death, was mentioned. No Jamaican, including Bogle, would find this acceptable. We came out of New World slavery as many people, now we are one. New World slavery and Africa should inspire us; we should not use them as crutches.

The white civil service system has never responded so quickly before to any of the needs of black people. Therefore, the reason for the proposed ban on our black identity must be seen as no better than the beads or bullets which were exchanged for slaves. We must insist that the choice to be who we say we are must remain and that black, white or any other identity must not be abolished, changed or tampered with again. It is almost unpardonable that our black identity, so dearly earned, can be put out to consultation by ignorant people. Such people should not be in charge of other people's freedom. A census that fails to capture, honestly, the human diversity of colour, class, race and creed cannot be used to monitor equality in any community.

Equality is dependent on identifying all the people of the community, so that their needs can be met. My colour is me and I shall not favour forms that exclude my black identity. It is evident that the civil servants involved are not aware of research that shows that a black identity is related to self-esteem and positive development. The arrogance with which this assault on black identity was carried out has done untold harm to race relations and the rights of black people. The idiot that calls me black, as an insult, does me no harm...I am black. The right to call ourselves black or white is already in place on national documents and must remain.

For the future, we must talk honestly about our identities and our histories (and this includes Chattel slavery) so that our children will learn that racial (colour) prejudice is the dangerous lie that damages us all.